Memoirs of Casanova Volume IV

Memoirs of Casanova Volume IV

Giacomo Casanova

MINT EDITIONS

Memoirs of Casanova Volume IV was first published in 1902.

This edition published by Mint Editions 2021.

ISBN 9781513281865 | E-ISBN 9781513286884

Published by Mint Editions®

**MINT
EDITIONS**

minteditionbooks.com

Publishing Director: Jennifer Newens
Design & Production: Rachel Lopez Metzger
Project Manager: Micaela Clark
Translated By: Arthur Machen
Typesetting: Westchester Publishing Services

Contents

I

A Fearful Misfortune Befalls Me—Love Cools Down—
Leave Corfu and Return to Venice—Give Up the Army and
Become a Fiddler

The wound was rapidly healing up, and I saw near at hand the
moment when Madame F—— would leave her bed, and resume
her usual avocations.

The governor of the galeasses having issued orders for a general
review at Gouyn, M. F——, left for that place in his galley, telling me
to join him there early on the following day with the felucca. I took
supper alone with Madame F——, and I told her how unhappy it made
me to remain one day away from her.

"Let us make up to-night for to-morrow's disappointment," she said,
"and let us spend it together in conversation. Here are the keys; when
you know that my maid has left me, come to me through my husband's
room."

I did not fail to follow her instructions to the letter, and we found
ourselves alone with five hours before us. It was the month of June, and
the heat was intense. She had gone to bed; I folded her in my arms, she
pressed me to her bosom, but, condemning herself to the most cruel
torture, she thought I had no right to complain, if I was subjected to
the same privation which she imposed upon herself. My remonstrances,
my prayers, my entreaties were of no avail.

"Love," she said, "must be kept in check with a tight hand, and we
can laugh at him, since, in spite of the tyranny which we force him to
obey, we succeed all the same in gratifying our desires."

After the first ecstasy, our eyes and lips unclosed together, and a little
apart from each other we take delight in seeing the mutual satisfaction
beaming on our features.

Our desires revive; she casts a look upon my state of innocence
entirely exposed to her sight. She seems vexed at my want of excitement,
and, throwing off everything which makes the heat unpleasant and
interferes with our pleasure, she bounds upon me. It is more than
amorous fury, it is desperate lust. I share her frenzy, I hug her with a
sort of delirium, I enjoy a felicity which is on the point of carrying me
to the regions of bliss. . . but, at the very moment of completing the

offering, she fails me, moves off, slips away, and comes back to work off my excitement with a hand which strikes me as cold as ice.

"Ah, thou cruel, beloved woman! Thou art burning with the fire of love, and thou deprivest thyself of the only remedy which could bring calm to thy senses! Thy lovely hand is more humane than thou art, but thou has not enjoyed the felicity that thy hand has given me. My hand must owe nothing to thine. Come, darling light of my heart, come! Love doubles my existence in the hope that I will die again, but only in that charming retreat from which you have ejected me in the very moment of my greatest enjoyment."

While I was speaking thus, her very soul was breathing forth the most tender sighs of happiness, and as she pressed me tightly in her arms I felt that she was weltering in an ocean of bliss.

Silence lasted rather a long time, but that unnatural felicity was imperfect, and increased my excitement.

"How canst thou complain," she said tenderly, "when it is to that very imperfection of our enjoyment that we are indebted for its continuance? I loved thee a few minutes since, now I love thee a thousand times more, and perhaps I should love thee less if thou hadst carried my enjoyment to its highest limit."

"Oh! how much art thou mistaken, lovely one! How great is thy error! Thou art feeding upon sophisms, and thou leavest reality aside; I mean nature which alone can give real felicity. Desires constantly renewed and never fully satisfied are more terrible than the torments of hell."

"But are not these desires happiness when they are always accompanied by hope?"

"No, if that hope is always disappointed. It becomes hell itself, because there is no hope, and hope must die when it is killed by constant deception."

"Dearest, if hope does not exist in hell, desires cannot be found there either; for to imagine desires without hopes would be more than madness."

"Well, answer me. If you desire to be mine entirely, and if you feel the hope of it, which, according to your way of reasoning, is a natural consequence, why do you always raise an impediment to your own hope? Cease, dearest, cease to deceive yourself by absurd sophisms. Let us be as happy as it is in nature to be, and be quite certain that the reality of happiness will increase our love, and that love will find a new life in our very enjoyment."

"What I see proves the contrary; you are alive with excitement now, but if your desires had been entirely satisfied, you would be dead, benumbed, motionless. I know it by experience: if you had breathed the full ecstacy of enjoyment, as you desired, you would have found a weak ardour only at long intervals."

"Ah! charming creature, your experience is but very small; do not trust to it. I see that you have never known love. That which you call love's grave is the sanctuary in which it receives life, the abode which makes it immortal. Give way to my prayers, my lovely friend, and then you shall know the difference between Love and Hymen. You shall see that, if Hymen likes to die in order to get rid of life, Love on the contrary expires only to spring up again into existence, and hastens to revive, so as to savour new enjoyment. Let me undeceive you, and believe me when I say that the full gratification of desires can only increase a hundredfold the mutual ardour of two beings who adore each other."

"Well, I must believe you; but let us wait. In the meantime let us enjoy all the trifles, all the sweet preliminaries of love. Devour thy mistress, dearest, but abandon to me all thy being. If this night is too short we must console ourselves to-morrow by making arrangements for another one."

"And if our intercourse should be discovered?"

"Do we make a mystery of it? Everybody can see that we love each other, and those who think that we do not enjoy the happiness of lovers are precisely the only persons we have to fear. We must only be careful to guard against being surprised in the very act of proving our love. Heaven and nature must protect our affection, for there is no crime when two hearts are blended in true love. Since I have been conscious of my own existence, Love has always seemed to me the god of my being, for every time I saw a man I was delighted; I thought that I was looking upon one-half of myself, because I felt I was made for him and he for me. I longed to be married. It was that uncertain longing of the heart which occupies exclusively a young girl of fifteen. I had no conception of love, but I fancied that it naturally accompanied marriage. You can therefore imagine my surprise when my husband, in the very act of making a woman of me, gave me a great deal of pain without giving me the slightest idea of pleasure! My imagination in the convent was much better than the reality I had been condemned to by my husband! The result has naturally been that we have become very good friends, but a very indifferent husband and wife, without any desires for each other. He has every reason to be pleased with me, for I always shew myself docile to his wishes, but enjoyment not being in those cases seasoned by love, he must find it without flavour, and he seldom comes to me for it.

"When I found out that you were in love with me, I felt delighted, and gave you every opportunity of becoming every day more deeply enamoured of me, thinking myself certain of never loving you myself. As soon as I felt that love had likewise attacked my heart, I ill-treated you to punish you for having made my heart sensible. Your patience and constancy have astonished me, and have caused me to be guilty, for after the first kiss I gave you I had no longer any control over myself. I was indeed astounded when I saw the havoc made by one single kiss, and I felt that my happiness was wrapped up in yours. That discovery flattered and delighted me, and I have found out, particularly to-night, that I cannot be happy unless you are so yourself."

"That is, my beloved, the most refined of all sentiments experienced by love, but it is impossible for you to render me completely happy without following in everything the laws and the wishes of nature."

The night was spent in tender discussions and in exquisite voluptuousness, and it was not without some grief that at day-break I tore myself from her arms to go to Gouyn. She wept for joy when she saw that I left her without having lost a particle of my vigour, for she did not imagine such a thing possible.

After that night, so rich in delights, ten or twelve days passed without giving us any opportunity of quenching even a small particle of the amorous thirst which devoured us, and it was then that a fearful misfortune befell me.

One evening after supper, M. D——R——having retired, M. F—— used no ceremony, and, although I was present, told his wife that he intended to pay her a visit after writing two letters which he had to dispatch early the next morning. The moment he had left the room we looked at each other, and with one accord fell into each other's arms. A torrent of delights rushed through our souls without restraint, without reserve, but when the first ardour had been appeased, without giving me time to think or to enjoy the most complete, the most delicious victory, she drew back, repulsed me, and threw herself, panting, distracted, upon a chair near her bed. Rooted to the spot, astonished, almost mad, I tremblingly looked at her, trying to understand what had caused such an extraordinary action. She turned round towards me and said, her eyes flashing with the fire of love,

"My darling, we were on the brink of the precipice."

"The precipice! Ah! cruel woman, you have killed me, I feel myself dying, and perhaps you will never see me again."

I left her in a state of frenzy, and rushed out, towards the esplanade, to cool myself, for I was choking. Any man who has not experienced the cruelty of an action like that of Madame F——, and especially in the situation I found myself in at that moment, mentally and bodily, can hardly realize what I suffered, and, although I have felt that suffering, I could not give an idea of it.

I was in that fearful state, when I heard my name called from a window, and unfortunately I condescended to answer. I went near the window, and I saw, thanks to the moonlight, the famous Melulla standing on her balcony.

"What are you doing there at this time of night?" I enquired.

"I am enjoying the cool evening breeze. Come up for a little while."

This Melulla, of fatal memory, was a courtezan from Zamte, of rare beauty, who for the last four months had been the delight and the rage of all the young men in Corfu. Those who had known her agreed in extolling her charms: she was the talk of all the city. I had seen her often, but, although she was very beautiful, I was very far from thinking her as lovely as Madame F——, putting my affection for the latter on one side. I recollect seeing in Dresden, in the year 1790, a very handsome woman who was the image of Melulla.

I went upstairs mechanically, and she took me to a voluptuous boudoir; she complained of my being the only one who had never paid her a visit, when I was the man she would have preferred to all others, and I had the infamy to give way. . . I became the most criminal of men.

It was neither desire, nor imagination, nor the merit of the woman which caused me to yield, for Melulla was in no way worthy of me; no, it was weakness, indolence, and the state of bodily and mental irritation in which I then found myself: it was a sort of spite, because the angel whom I adored had displeased me by a caprice, which, had I not been unworthy of her, would only have caused me to be still more attached to her.

Melulla, highly pleased with her success, refused the gold I wanted to give her, and allowed me to go after I had spent two hours with her.

When I recovered my composure, I had but one feeling-hatred for myself and for the contemptible creature who had allured me to be guilty of so vile an insult to the loveliest of her sex. I went home the prey to fearful remorse, and went to bed, but sleep never closed my eyes throughout that cruel night.

In the morning, worn out with fatigue and sorrow, I got up, and as soon as I was dressed I went to M. F——, who had sent for me to give me some orders. After I had returned, and had given him an account of my mission, I called upon Madame F——, and finding her at her toilet I wished her good morning, observing that her lovely face was breathing the cheerfulness and the calm of happiness; but, suddenly, her eyes meeting mine, I saw her countenance change, and an expression of sadness replace her looks of satisfaction. She cast her eyes down as if she was deep in thought, raised them again as if to read my very soul, and breaking our painful silence, as soon as she had dismissed her maid, she said to me, with an accent full of tenderness and of solemnity,

"Dear one, let there be no concealment either on my part or on yours. I felt deeply grieved when I saw you leave me last night, and a little consideration made me understand all the evil which might accrue to you in consequence of what I had done. With a nature like yours, such scenes might cause very dangerous disorders, and I have resolved not to do again anything by halves. I thought that you went out to breathe the fresh air, and I hoped it would do you good. I placed myself at my window, where I remained more than an hour without seeing alight in your room. Sorry for what I had done, loving you more than ever, I was compelled, when my husband came to my room, to go to bed with the sad conviction that you had not come home. This morning, M. F. sent an officer to tell you that he wanted to see you, and I heard the messenger inform him that you were not yet up, and that you had come home very late. I felt my heart swell with sorrow. I am not jealous, dearest, for I know that you cannot love anyone but me; I only felt afraid of some misfortune. At last, this morning, when I heard you coming, I was happy, because I was ready to skew my repentance, but I looked at you, and you seemed a different man. Now, I am still looking at you, and, in spite of myself, my soul reads upon your countenance that you are guilty, that you have outraged my love. Tell me at once, dearest, if I am mistaken; if you have deceived me, say so openly. Do not be unfaithful to love and to truth. Knowing that I was the cause of it, I should never forgive my self, but there is an excuse for you in my heart, in my whole being."

More than once, in the course of my life, I have found myself under the painful necessity of telling falsehoods to the woman I loved; but in this case, after so true, so touching an appeal, how could I be otherwise than sincere? I felt myself sufficiently debased by my crime, and I could not degrade myself still more by falsehood. I was so far from being disposed to such a line of conduct that I could not speak, and I burst out crying.

"What, my darling! you are weeping! Your tears make me miserable. You ought not to have shed any with me but tears of happiness and love. Quick, my beloved, tell me whether you have made me wretched. Tell me what fearful revenge you have taken on me, who would rather die than offend you. If I have caused you any sorrow, it has been in the innocence of a loving and devoted heart."

"My own darling angel, I never thought of revenge, for my heart, which can never cease to adore you, could never conceive such a dreadful idea. It is against my own heart that my cowardly weakness has allured me to the commission of a crime which, for the remainder of my life, makes me unworthy of you."

"Have you, then, given yourself to some wretched woman?"

"Yes, I have spent two hours in the vilest debauchery, and my soul was present only to be the witness of my sadness, of my remorse, of my unworthiness."

"Sadness and remorse! Oh, my poor friend! I believe it. But it is my fault; I alone ought to suffer; it is I who must beg you to forgive me."

Her tears made mine flow again.

"Divine soul," I said, "the reproaches you are addressing to yourself increase twofold the gravity of my crime. You would never have been guilty of any wrong against me if I had been really worthy of your love."

I felt deeply the truth of my words.

We spent the remainder of the day apparently quiet and composed, concealing our sadness in the depths of our hearts. She was curious to know all the circumstances of my miserable adventure, and, accepting it as an expiation, I related them to her. Full of kindness, she assured me that we were bound to ascribe that accident to fate, and that the same thing might have happened to the best of men. She added that I was more to be pitied than condemned, and that she did not love me less. We both were certain that we would seize the first favourable opportunity, she of obtaining her pardon, I of atoning for my crime, by giving each other new and complete proofs of our mutual ardour. But Heaven in its justice had ordered differently, and I was cruelly punished for my disgusting debauchery.

On the third day, as I got up in the morning, an awful pricking announced the horrid state into which the wretched Melulla had thrown me. I was thunderstruck! And when I came to think of the misery which I might have caused if, during the last three days, I had obtained some new favour from my lovely mistress, I was on the point of going mad. What would have been her feelings if I had made her unhappy for the remainder of her life! Would anyone, then, knowing the whole case, have condemned me if I had destroyed my own life in order to deliver myself from everlasting remorse? No, for the man who kills himself from sheer despair, thus performing upon himself the execution of the sentence he would have deserved at the hands of justice cannot be blamed either by a virtuous philosopher or by a tolerant Christian. But of one thing I am quite certain: if such a misfortune had happened, I should have committed suicide.

Overwhelmed with grief by the discovery I had just made, but thinking that I should get rid of the inconvenience as I had done three times before, I prepared myself for a strict diet, which would restore my health in six weeks without anyone having any suspicion of my illness, but I soon found out that I had not seen the end of my troubles; Melulla had communicated to my system all the poisons which corrupt the source of life. I was acquainted with an elderly doctor of great experience in those matters; I consulted him, and he promised to set me to rights in two months; he proved as good as his word. At the beginning of September I found myself in good health, and it was about that time that I returned to Venice.

The first thing I resolved on, as soon as I discovered the state I was in, was to confess everything to Madame F——. I did not wish to wait for the time when a compulsory confession would have made her blush for her weakness, and given her cause to think of the fearful consequences which might have been the result of her passion for me. Her affection was too dear to me to run the risk of losing it through a want of confidence in her. Knowing her heart, her candour, and the generosity which had prompted her to say that I was more to be pitied than blamed, I thought myself bound to prove by my sincerity that I deserved her esteem.

I told her candidly my position and the state I had been thrown in, when I thought of the dreadful consequences it might have had for her. I saw her shudder and tremble, and she turned pale with fear when I added that I would have avenged her by killing myself.

"Villainous, infamous Melulla!" she exclaimed.

And I repeated those words, but turning them against myself when I realized all I had sacrificed through the most disgusting weakness.

Everyone in Corfu knew of my visit to the wretched Melulla, and everyone seemed surprised to see the appearance of health on my countenance; for many were the victims that she had treated like me.

My illness was not my only sorrow; I had others which, although of a different nature, were not less serious. It was written in the book of fate that I should return to Venice a simple ensign as when I left: the general did not keep his word, and the bastard son of a nobleman was promoted to the lieutenancy instead of myself. From that moment the military profession, the one most subject to arbitrary despotism, inspired me with disgust, and I determined to give it up. But I had another still more important motive for sorrow in the fickleness of fortune which had completely turned against me. I remarked that, from the time of my degradation with Melulla, every kind of misfortune befell me. The greatest of all—that which I felt most, but which I had the good sense to try and consider a favour—was that a week before the departure of the army M. D——R—— took me again for his adjutant, and M. F—— had to engage another in my place. On the occasion of that change Madame F told me, with an appearance of regret, that in Venice we could not, for many reasons, continue our intimacy. I begged her to spare me the reasons, as I foresaw that they would only throw humiliation upon me. I began to discover that the goddess I had worshipped was, after all, a poor human being like all other women, and to think that I should have been very foolish to give up my life for her. I probed in one day the real worth of her heart, for she told me, I cannot recollect in reference to what, that I excited her pity. I saw clearly that she no longer loved me; pity is a debasing feeling which cannot find a home in a heart full of love, for that dreary sentiment is too near a relative of contempt. Since that time I never found myself alone with Madame F——. I loved her still; I could easily have made her blush, but I did not do it.

As soon as we reached Venice she became attached to M. F—— R——, whom she loved until death took him from her. She was unhappy enough to lose her sight twenty years after. I believe she is still alive.

During the last two months of my stay in Corfu, I learned the most bitter and important lessons. In after years I often derived useful hints from the experience I acquired at that time.

Before my adventure with the worthless Melulla, I enjoyed good health, I was rich, lucky at play, liked by everybody, beloved by the most lovely woman of Corfu. When I spoke, everybody would listen and admire my wit; my words were taken for oracles, and everyone coincided with me in everything. After my fatal meeting with the courtezan I rapidly lost my health, my money, my credit; cheerfulness, consideration, wit, everything, even the faculty of eloquence vanished with fortune. I would talk, but people knew that I was unfortunate, and I no longer interested or convinced my hearers. The influence I had over Madame F——faded away little by little, and, almost without her knowing it, the lovely woman became completely indifferent to me.

I left Corfu without money, although I had sold or pledged everything I had of any value. Twice I had reached Corfu rich and happy, twice I left it poor and miserable. But this time I had contracted debts which I have never paid, not through want of will but through carelessness.

Rich and in good health, everyone received me with open arms; poor and looking sick, no one shewed me any consideration. With a full purse and the tone of a conqueror, I was thought witty, amusing; with an empty purse and a modest air, all I said appeared dull and insipid. If I had become rich again, how soon I would have been again accounted the eighth wonder of the world! Oh, men! oh, fortune! Everyone avoided me as if the ill luck which crushed me down was infectious.

We left Corfu towards the end of September, with five galleys, two galeasses, and several smaller vessels, under the command of M. Renier. We sailed along the shores of the Adriatic, towards the north of the gulf, where there are a great many harbours, and we put in one of them every night. I saw Madame F——every evening; she always came with her husband to take supper on board our galeass. We had a fortunate voyage, and cast anchor in the harbour of Venice on the 14th of October, 1745, and after having performed quarantine on board our ships, we landed on the 25th of November. Two months afterwards, the galeasses were set aside altogether. The use of these vessels could be traced very far back in ancient times; their maintenance was very expensive, and they were useless. A galeass had the frame of a frigate with the rowing apparatus of the galley, and when there was no wind, five hundred slaves had to row.

Before simple good sense managed to prevail and to enforce the suppression of these useless carcasses, there were long discussions in the senate, and those who opposed the measure took their principal ground of opposition in the necessity of respecting and conserving all the institutions of olden times. That is the disease of persons who can never identify themselves with the successive improvements born of reason and experience; worthy persons who ought to be sent to China, or to the dominions of the Grand Lama, where they would certainly be more at home than in Europe.

That ground of opposition to all improvements, however absurd it may be, is a very powerful one in a republic, which must tremble at the mere idea of novelty either in important or in trifling things. Superstition has likewise a great part to play in these conservative views.

There is one thing that the Republic of Venice will never alter: I mean the galleys, because the Venetians truly require such vessels to ply, in all weathers and in spite of the frequent calms, in a narrow sea, and because they would not know what to do with the men sentenced to hard labour.

I have observed a singular thing in Corfu, where there are often as many as three thousand galley slaves; it is that the men who row on the galleys, in consequence of a sentence passed upon them for some crime, are held in a kind of opprobrium, whilst those who are there voluntarily are, to some extent, respected. I have always thought it ought to be the reverse, because misfortune, whatever it may be, ought to inspire some sort of respect; but the vile fellow who condemns himself voluntarily and as a trade to the position of a slave seems to me contemptible in the highest degree. The convicts of the Republic, however, enjoy many privileges, and are, in every way, better treated than the soldiers. It very often occurs that soldiers desert and give themselves up to a 'sopracomito' to become galley slaves. In those cases, the captain who loses a soldier has nothing to do but to submit patiently, for he would claim the man in vain. The reason of it is that the Republic has always believed galley slaves more necessary than soldiers. The Venetians may perhaps now (I am writing these lines in the year 1797) begin to realize their mistake.

A galley slave, for instance, has the privilege of stealing with impunity. It is considered that stealing is the least crime they can be guilty of, and that they ought to be forgiven for it.

"Keep on your guard," says the master of the galley slave; "and if you catch him in the act of stealing, thrash him, but be careful not to cripple him; otherwise you must pay me the one hundred ducats the man has cost me."

A court of justice could not have a galley slave taken from a galley, without paying the master the amount he has disbursed for the man.

As soon as I had landed in Venice, I called upon Madame Orio, but I found the house empty. A neighbour told me that she had married the Procurator Rosa, and had removed to his house. I went immediately to M. Rosa and was well received. Madame Orio informed me that Nanette had become Countess R., and was living in Guastalla with her husband.

Twenty-four years afterwards, I met her eldest son, then a distinguished officer in the service of the Infante of Parma.

As for Marton, the grace of Heaven had touched her, and she had become a nun in the convent at Muran. Two years afterwards, I received from her a letter full of unction, in which she adjured me, in the name of Our Saviour and of the Holy Virgin, never to present myself before her eyes. She added that she was bound by Christian charity to forgive me for the crime I had committed in seducing her, and she felt certain of the reward of the elect, and she assured me that she would ever pray earnestly for my conversion.

I never saw her again, but she saw me in 1754, as I will mention when we reach that year.

I found Madame Manzoni still the same. She had predicted that I would not remain in the military profession, and when I told her that I had made up my mind to give it up, because I could not be reconciled to the injustice I had experienced, she burst out laughing. She enquired about the profession I intended to follow after giving up the army, and I answered that I wished to become an advocate. She laughed again, saying that it was too late. Yet I was only twenty years old.

When I called upon M. Grimani I had a friendly welcome from him, but, having enquired after my brother Francois, he told me that he had had him confined in Fort Saint Andre, the same to which I had been sent before the arrival of the Bishop of Martorano.

"He works for the major there," he said; "he copies Simonetti's battle-pieces, and the major pays him for them; in that manner he earns his living, and is becoming a good painter."

"But he is not a prisoner?"

"Well, very much like it, for he cannot leave the fort. The major, whose name is Spiridion, is a friend of Razetta, who could not refuse him the pleasure of taking care of your brother."

I felt it a dreadful curse that the fatal Razetta should be the tormentor of all my family, but I concealed my anger.

"Is my sister," I enquired, "still with him?"

"No, she has gone to your mother in Dresden."

This was good news.

I took a cordial leave of the Abbe Grimani, and I proceeded to Fort Saint Andre. I found my brother hard at work, neither pleased nor displeased with his position, and enjoying good health. After embracing him affectionately, I enquired what crime he had committed to be thus a prisoner.

"Ask the major," he said, "for I have not the faintest idea."

The major came in just then, so I gave him the military salute, and asked by what authority he kept my brother under arrest.

"I am not accountable to you for my actions."

"That remains to be seen."

I then told my brother to take his hat, and to come and dine with me. The major laughed, and said that he had no objection provided the sentinel allowed him to pass.

I saw that I should only waste my time in discussion, and I left the fort fully bent on obtaining justice.

The next day I went to the war office, where I had the pleasure of meeting my dear Major Pelodoro, who was then commander of the Fortress of Chiozza. I informed him of the complaint I wanted to prefer before the secretary of war respecting my brother's arrest, and of the resolution I had taken to leave the army. He promised me that, as soon as the consent of the secretary for war could be obtained, he would find a purchaser for my commission at the same price I had paid for it.

I had not long to wait. The war secretary came to the office, and everything was settled in half an hour. He promised his consent to the sale of my commission as soon as he ascertained the abilities of the purchaser, and Major Spiridion happening to make his appearance in the office while I was still there, the secretary ordered him rather angrily, to set my brother at liberty immediately, and cautioned him not to be guilty again of such reprehensible and arbitrary acts.

I went at once for my brother, and we lived together in furnished lodgings.

A few days afterwards, having received my discharge and one hundred sequins, I threw off my uniform, and found myself once more my own master.

I had to earn my living in one way or another, and I decided for the profession of gamester. But Dame Fortune was not of the same opinion, for she refused to smile upon me from the very first step I took in the career, and in less than a week I did not possess a groat. What was to become of me? One must live, and I turned fiddler. Doctor Gozzi had taught me well enough to enable me to scrape on the violin in the orchestra of a theatre, and having mentioned my wishes to M. Grimani he procured me an engagement at his own theatre of Saint Samuel, where I earned a crown a day, and supported myself while I awaited better things.

Fully aware of my real position, I never shewed myself in the fashionable circles which I used to frequent before my fortune had sunk so low. I knew that I was considered as a worthless fellow, but I did not care. People despised me, as a matter of course; but I found comfort in the consciousness that I was worthy of contempt. I felt humiliated by the position to which I was reduced after having played so brilliant a part in society; but as I kept the secret to myself I was not degraded, even if I felt some shame. I had not exchanged my last word with Dame Fortune, and was still in hope of reckoning with her some day, because I was young, and youth is dear to Fortune.

II

I Turn Out A Worthless Fellow—My Good Fortune—I Become A Rich Nobleman

With an education which ought to have ensured me an honourable standing in the world, with some intelligence, wit, good literary and scientific knowledge, and endowed with those accidental physical qualities which are such a good passport into society, I found myself, at the age of twenty, the mean follower of a sublime art, in which, if great talent is rightly admired, mediocrity is as rightly despised. I was compelled by poverty to become a member of a musical band, in which I could expect neither esteem nor consideration, and I was well aware that I should be the laughing-stock of the persons who had known me as a doctor in divinity, as an ecclesiastic, and as an officer in the army, and had welcomed me in the highest society.

I knew all that, for I was not blind to my position; but contempt, the only thing to which I could not have remained indifferent, never shewed itself anywhere under a form tangible enough for me to have no doubt of my being despised, and I set it at defiance, because I was satisfied that contempt is due only to cowardly, mean actions, and I was conscious that I had never been guilty of any. As to public esteem, which I had ever been anxious to secure, my ambition was slumbering, and satisfied with being my own master I enjoyed my independence without puzzling my head about the future. I felt that in my first profession, as I was not blessed with the vocation necessary to it, I should have succeeded only by dint of hypocrisy, and I should have been despicable in my own estimation, even if I had seen the purple mantle on my shoulders, for the greatest dignities cannot silence a man's own conscience. If, on the other hand, I had continued to seek fortune in a military career, which is surrounded by a halo of glory, but is otherwise the worst of professions for the constant self-abnegation, for the complete surrender of one's will which passive obedience demands, I should have required a patience to which I could not lay any claim, as every kind of injustice was revolting to me, and as I could not bear to feel myself dependent. Besides, I was of opinion that a man's profession, whatever it might be, ought to supply him with enough money to satisfy all his wants; and the very poor pay of an officer would never have been sufficient to cover my expenses, because my education had given me greater wants than those of officers in general. By scraping my violin I earned enough to keep myself without requiring anybody's assistance, and I have always thought that the man who can support himself is happy. I grant that my profession was not a brilliant one, but I did not mind it, and, calling prejudices all the feelings which rose in my breast against myself, I was not long in sharing all the habits of my degraded comrades. When the play was over, I went with them to the drinking-booth, which we often left intoxicated to spend the night in houses of ill-fame. When we happened to find those places already tenanted by other men, we forced them by violence to quit the premises, and defrauded the miserable victims of prostitution of the mean salary the law allows them, after compelling them to yield to our brutality. Our scandalous proceedings often exposed us to the greatest danger.

We would very often spend the whole night rambling about the city, inventing and carrying into execution the most impertinent, practical jokes. One of our favourite pleasures was to unmoor the patricians' gondolas, and to let them float at random along the canals, enjoying by anticipation all the curses that gondoliers would not fail to indulge in. We would rouse up hurriedly, in the middle of the night, an honest midwife, telling her to hasten to Madame So-and-so, who, not being even pregnant, was sure to tell her she was a fool when she called at the house. We did the same with physicians, whom we often sent half dressed to some nobleman who was enjoying excellent health. The priests fared no better; we would send them to carry the last sacraments to married men who were peacefully slumbering near their wives, and not thinking of extreme unction.

We were in the habit of cutting the wires of the bells in every house, and if we chanced to find a gate open we would go up the stairs in the dark, and frighten the sleeping inmates by telling them very loudly that the house door was not closed, after which we would go down, making as much noise as we could, and leave the house with the gate wide open.

During a very dark night we formed a plot to overturn the large marble table of St. Angelo's Square, on which it was said that in the days of the League of Cambray the commissaries of the Republic were in the habit of paying the bounty to the recruits who engaged to fight under the standard of St. Mark—a circumstance which secured for the table a sort of public veneration.

Whenever we could contrive to get into a church tower we thought it great fun to frighten all the parish by ringing the alarm bell, as if some fire had broken out; but that was not all, we always cut the bell ropes, so that in the morning the churchwardens had no means of summoning the faithful to early mass. Sometimes we would cross the canal, each of us in a different gondola, and take to our heels without paying as soon as we landed on the opposite side, in order to make the gondoliers run after us.

The city was alive with complaints, and we laughed at the useless search made by the police to find out those who disturbed the peace of the inhabitants. We took good care to be careful, for if we had been discovered we stood a very fair chance of being sent to practice rowing at the expense of the Council of Ten.

We were seven, and sometimes eight, because, being much attached to my brother Francois, I gave him a share now and then in our nocturnal orgies. But at last fear put a stop to our criminal jokes, which in those days I used to call only the frolics of young men. This is the amusing adventure which closed our exploits.

In every one of the seventy-two parishes of the city of Venice, there is a large public-house called 'magazzino'. It remains open all night, and wine is retailed there at a cheaper price than in all the other drinking houses. People can likewise eat in the 'magazzino', but they must obtain what they want from the pork butcher near by, who has the exclusive sale of eatables, and likewise keeps his shop open throughout the night. The pork butcher is usually a very poor cook, but as he is cheap, poor people are willingly satisfied with him, and these resorts are considered very useful to the lower class. The nobility, the merchants, even workmen in good circumstances, are never seen in the 'magazzino', for cleanliness is not exactly worshipped in such places. Yet there are a few private rooms which contain a table surrounded with benches, in which a respectable family or a few friends can enjoy themselves in a decent way.

It was during the Carnival of 1745, after midnight; we were, all the eight of us, rambling about together with our masks on, in quest of some new sort of mischief to amuse us, and we went into the magazzino of the parish of the Holy Cross to get something to drink. We found the public room empty, but in one of the private chambers we discovered three men quietly conversing with a young and pretty woman, and enjoying their wine.

Our chief, a noble Venetian belonging to the Balbi family, said to us, "It would be a good joke to carry off those three blockheads, and to keep the pretty woman in our possession." He immediately explained his plan, and under cover of our masks we entered their room, Balbi at the head of us. Our sudden appearance rather surprised the good people, but you may fancy their astonishment when they heard Balbi say to them: "Under penalty of death, and by order of the Council of Ten, I command you to follow us immediately, without making the slightest noise; as to you, my good woman, you need not be frightened, you will be escorted to your house." When he had finished his speech, two of us got hold of the woman to take her where our chief had arranged beforehand, and the others seized the three poor fellows, who were trembling all over, and had not the slightest idea of opposing any resistance.

The waiter of the magazzino came to be paid, and our chief gave him what was due, enjoining silence under penalty of death. We took our three prisoners to a large boat. Balbi went to the stern, ordered the boatman to stand at the bow, and told him that he need not enquire where we were going, that he would steer himself whichever way he thought fit. Not one of us knew where Balbi wanted to take the three poor devils.

He sails all along the canal, gets out of it, takes several turnings, and in a quarter of an hour, we reach Saint George where Balbi lands our prisoners, who are delighted to find themselves at liberty. After this, the boatman is ordered to take us to Saint Genevieve, where we land, after paying for the boat.

We proceed at once to Palombo Square, where my brother and another of our band were waiting for us with our lovely prisoner, who was crying.

"Do not weep, my beauty," says Balbi to her, "we will not hurt you. We intend only to take some refreshment at the Rialto, and then we will take you home in safety."

"Where is my husband?"

"Never fear; you shall see him again to-morrow."

Comforted by that promise, and as gentle as a lamb, she follows us to the "Two Swords." We ordered a good fire in a private room, and, everything we wanted to eat and to drink having been brought in, we send the waiter away, and remain alone. We take off our masks, and the sight of eight young, healthy faces seems to please the beauty we had so unceremoniously carried off. We soon manage to reconcile her to her fate by the gallantry of our proceedings; encouraged by a good supper and by the stimulus of wine, prepared by our compliments and by a few kisses, she realizes what is in store for her, and does not seem to have any unconquerable objection. Our chief, as a matter of right, claims the privilege of opening the ball; and by dint of sweet words he overcomes the very natural repugnance she feels at consummating the sacrifice in so numerous company. She, doubtless, thinks the offering agreeable, for, when I present myself as the priest appointed to sacrifice a second time to the god of love, she receives me almost with gratitude, and she cannot conceal her joy when she finds out that she is destined to make us all happy. My brother Francois alone exempted himself from paying the tribute, saying that he was ill, the only excuse which could render his refusal valid, for we had established as a law that every member of our society was bound to do whatever was done by the others.

After that fine exploit, we put on our masks, and, the bill being paid, escorted the happy victim to Saint Job, where she lived, and did not leave her till we had seen her safe in her house, and the street door closed.

My readers may imagine whether we felt inclined to laugh when the charming creature bade us good night, thanking us all with perfect good faith!

Two days afterwards, our nocturnal orgy began to be talked of. The young woman's husband was a weaver by trade, and so were his two friends. They joined together to address a complaint to the Council of Ten. The complaint was candidly written and contained nothing but the truth, but the criminal portion of the truth was veiled by a circumstance which must have brought a smile on the grave countenances of the judges, and highly amused the public at large: the complaint setting forth that the eight masked men had not rendered themselves guilty of any act disagreeable to the wife. It went on to say that the two men who had carried her off had taken her to such a place, where they had, an hour later, been met by the other six, and that they had all repaired to the "Two Swords," where they had spent an hour in drinking. The said lady having been handsomely entertained by the eight masked men, had been escorted to her house, where she had been politely requested to excuse the joke perpetrated upon her husband. The three plaintiffs had not been able to leave the island of Saint George until day-break, and the husband, on reaching his house, had found his wife quietly asleep in her bed. She had informed him of all that had happened; she complained of nothing but of the great fright she had experienced on account of her husband,

and on that count she entreated justice and the punishment of the guilty parties.

That complaint was comic throughout, for the three rogues shewed themselves very brave in writing, stating that they would certainly not have given way so easily if the dread authority of the council had not been put forth by the leader of the band. The document produced three different results; in the first place, it amused the town; in the second, all the idlers of Venice went to Saint Job to hear the account of the adventure from the lips of the heroine herself, and she got many presents from her numerous visitors; in the third place, the Council of Ten offered a reward of five hundred ducats to any person giving such information as would lead to the arrest of the perpetrators of the practical joke, even if the informer belonged to the band, provided he was not the leader.

The offer of that reward would have made us tremble if our leader, precisely the one who alone had no interest in turning informer, had not been a patrician. The rank of Balbi quieted my anxiety at once, because I knew that, even supposing one of us were vile enough to betray our secret for the sake of the reward, the tribunal would have done nothing in order not to implicate a patrician. There was no cowardly traitor amongst us, although we were all poor; but fear had its effect, and our nocturnal pranks were not renewed.

Three or four months afterwards the chevalier Nicolas Iron, then one of the inquisitors, astonished me greatly by telling me the whole story, giving the names of all the actors. He did not tell me whether any one of the band had betrayed the secret, and I did not care to know; but I could clearly see the characteristic spirit of the aristocracy, for which the 'solo mihi' is the supreme law.

Towards the middle of April of the year 1746 M. Girolamo Cornaro, the eldest son of the family Cornaro de la Reine, married a daughter of the house of Soranzo de St. Pol, and I had the honour of being present at the wedding—as a fiddler. I played the violin in one of the numerous bands engaged for the balls which were given for three consecutive days in the Soranzo Palace.

On the third day, towards the end of the dancing, an hour before day-break, feeling tired, I left the orchestra abruptly; and as I was going down the stairs I observed a senator, wearing his red robes, on the point of getting into a gondola. In taking his handkerchief out of his pocket he let a letter drop on the ground. I picked it up, and coming up to him just as he was going down the steps I handed it to him. He received it with many thanks, and enquired where I lived. I told him, and he insisted upon my coming with him in the gondola saying that he would leave me at my house. I accepted gratefully, and sat down near him. A few minutes afterwards he asked me to rub his left arm, which, he said, was so benumbed that he could not feel it. I rubbed it with all my strength, but he told me in a sort of indistinct whisper that the numbness was spreading all along the left side, and that he was dying.

I was greatly frightened; I opened the curtain, took the lantern, and found him almost insensible, and the mouth drawn on one side. I understood that he was seized with an apoplectic stroke, and called out to the gondoliers to land me at once, in order to procure a surgeon to bleed the patient.

I jumped out of the gondola, and found myself on the very spot where three years before I had taught Razetta such a forcible lesson; I enquired for a surgeon at the first coffee-house, and ran to the house that was pointed out to me. I knocked as hard as I could; the door was at last opened, and I made the surgeon follow me in his dressing-gown as far as the gondola, which was waiting; he bled the senator while I was tearing my shirt to make the compress and the bandage.

The operation being performed, I ordered the gondoliers to row as fast as possible, and we soon reached St. Marina; the servants were roused up, and taking the sick man out of the gondola we carried him to his bed almost dead.

Taking everything upon myself, I ordered a servant to hurry out for a physician, who came in a short time, and ordered the patient to be bled again, thus approving the first bleeding prescribed by me. Thinking I had a right to watch the sick man, I settled myself near his bed to give him every care he required.

An hour later, two noblemen, friends of the senator, came in, one a few minutes after the other. They were in despair; they had enquired about the accident from the gondoliers, and having been told that I knew more than they did, they loaded me with questions which I answered. They did not know who I was, and did not like to ask me; whilst I thought it better to preserve a modest silence.

The patient did not move; his breathing alone shewed that he was still alive; fomentations were constantly applied, and the priest who had been sent for, and was of very little use under such circumstances, seemed to be there only to see him die. All visitors were sent away by my advice, and the two noblemen and myself were the only persons in the sick man's room. At noon we partook silently of some dinner which was served in the sick room.

In the evening one of the two friends told me that if I had any business to attend to I could go, because they would both pass the night on a mattress near the patient.

"And I, sir," I said, "will remain near his bed in this arm-chair, for if I went away the patient would die, and he will live as long as I am near him."

This sententious answer struck them with astonishment, as I expected it would, and they looked at each other in great surprise.

We had supper, and in the little conversation we had I gathered the information that the senator, their friend, was M. de Bragadin, the only brother of the procurator of that name. He was celebrated in Venice not only for his eloquence and his great talents as a statesman, but also for the gallantries of his youth. He had been very extravagant with women, and more than one of them had committed many follies for him. He had gambled and lost a great deal, and his brother was his most bitter enemy, because he was infatuated with the idea that he had tried to poison him. He had accused him of that crime before the Council of Ten, which, after an investigation of eight months, had brought in a verdict of not guilty: but that just sentence, although given unanimously by that high tribunal, had not had the effect of destroying his brother's prejudices against him.

M. de Bragadin, who was perfectly innocent of such a crime and oppressed by an unjust brother who deprived him of half of his income, spent his days like an amiable philosopher, surrounded by his friends, amongst whom were the two noblemen who were then watching him; one belonged to the Dandolo family, the other was a Barbaro, and both were excellent men. M. de Bragadin was handsome, learned, cheerful, and most kindly disposed; he was then about fifty years old.

The physician who attended him was named Terro; he thought, by some peculiar train of reasoning, that he could cure him by applying a mercurial ointment to the chest, to which no one raised any objection. The rapid effect of the remedy delighted the two friends, but it frightened me, for in less than twenty-four hours the patient was labouring under great excitement of the brain. The physician said that he had expected that effect, but that on the following day the remedy would act less on the brain, and diffuse its beneficial action through the whole of the system, which required to be invigorated by a proper equilibrium in the circulation of the fluids.

At midnight the patient was in a state of high fever, and in a fearful state of irritation. I examined him closely, and found him hardly able to breathe. I roused up his two friends; and declared that in my opinion the patient would soon die unless the fatal ointment was at once removed. And without waiting for their answer, I bared his chest, took off the plaster, washed the skin carefully with lukewarm water, and in less than three minutes he breathed freely and fell into a quiet sleep. Delighted with such a fortunate result, we lay down again.

The physician came very early in the morning, and was much pleased to see his patient so much better, but when M. Dandolo informed him of what had been done, he was angry, said it was enough to kill his patient, and asked who had been so audacious as to destroy the effect of his prescription. M. de Bragadin, speaking for the first time, said to him—

"Doctor, the person who has delivered me from your mercury, which was killing me, is a more skilful physician than you;" and, saying these words, he pointed to me.

It would be hard to say who was the more astonished: the doctor, when he saw an unknown young man, whom he must have taken for an impostor, declared more learned than himself; or I, when I saw myself transformed into a physician, at a moment's notice. I kept silent, looking very modest, but hardly able to control my mirth, whilst the doctor was staring at me with a mixture of astonishment and of spite, evidently thinking me some bold quack who had tried to supplant him. At last, turning towards M. de Bragadin, he told him coldly that he would leave him in my hands; he was taken at his word, he went away, and behold! I had become the physician of one of the most illustrious members of the Venetian Senate! I must confess that I was very glad of it, and I told my patient that a proper diet was all he needed, and that nature, assisted by the approaching fine season, would do the rest.

The dismissed physician related the affair through the town, and, as M. de Bragadin was rapidly improving, one of his relations, who came to see him, told him that everybody was astonished at his having chosen for his physician a fiddler from the theatre; but the senator put a stop to his remarks by answering that a fiddler could know more than all the doctors in Venice, and that he owed his life to me.

The worthy nobleman considered me as his oracle, and his two friends listened to me with the deepest attention. Their infatuation encouraging me, I spoke like a learned physician, I dogmatized, I quoted authors whom I had never read.

M. de Bragadin, who had the weakness to believe in the occult sciences, told me one day that, for a young man of my age, he thought my learning too extensive, and that he was certain I was the possessor of some supernatural endowment. He entreated me to tell him the truth.

What extraordinary things will sometimes occur from mere chance, or from the force of circumstances! Unwilling to hurt his vanity by telling him that he was mistaken, I took the wild resolution of informing him, in the presence of his two friends, that I possessed a certain numeral calculus which gave answers (also in numbers), to any questions I liked to put.

M. de Bragadin said that it was Solomon's key, vulgarly called cabalistic science, and he asked me from whom I learnt it.

"From an old hermit," I answered, "who lives on the Carpegna Mountain, and whose acquaintance I made quite by chance when I was a prisoner in the Spanish army."

"The hermit," remarked the senator, "has without informing you of it, linked an invisible spirit to the calculus he has taught you, for simple numbers can not have the power of reason. You possess a real treasure, and you may derive great advantages from it."

"I do not know," I said, "in what way I could make my science useful, because the answers given by the numerical figures are often so obscure that I have felt discouraged, and I very seldom tried to make any use of my calculus. Yet, it is very true that, if I had not formed my pyramid, I never should have had the happiness of knowing your excellency."

"How so?"

"On the second day, during the festivities at the Soranzo Palace, I enquired of my oracle whether I would meet at the ball anyone whom I should not care to see. The answer I obtained was this: 'Leave the ball-room precisely at four o'clock.' I obeyed implicitly, and met your excellency."

The three friends were astounded. M. Dandolo asked me whether I would answer a question he would ask, the interpretation of which would belong only to him, as he was the only person acquainted with the subject of the question.

I declared myself quite willing, for it was necessary to brazen it out, after having ventured as far as I had done. He wrote the question, and gave it to me; I read it, I could not understand either the subject or the meaning of the words, but it did not matter, I had to give an answer. If the question was so obscure that I could not make out the sense of it, it was natural that I should not understand the answer. I therefore answered, in ordinary figures, four lines of which he alone could be the interpreter, not caring much, at least in appearance, how they would be understood. M. Dandolo read them twice over, seemed astonished, said that it was all very plain to him; it was Divine, it was unique, it was a gift from Heaven, the numbers being only the vehicle, but the answer emanating evidently from an immortal spirit.

M. Dandolo was so well pleased that his two friends very naturally wanted also to make an experiment. They asked questions on all sorts of subjects, and my answers, perfectly unintelligible to myself, were all held as Divine by them. I congratulated them on their success, and congratulated myself in their presence upon being the possessor of a thing to which I had until then attached no importance whatever, but which I promised to cultivate carefully, knowing that I could thus be of some service to their excellencies.

They all asked me how long I would require to teach them the rules of my sublime calculus. "Not very long," I answered, "and I will teach you as you wish, although the hermit assured me that I would die suddenly within three days if I communicated my science to anyone, but I have no faith whatever in that prediction." M. de Bragadin who believed in it more than I did, told me in a serious tone that I was bound to have faith in it, and from that day they never asked me again to teach them. They very likely thought that, if they could attach me to them, it would answer the purpose as well as if they possessed the science themselves. Thus I became the hierophant of those three worthy and talented men, who, in spite of their literary accomplishments, were not wise, since they were infatuated with occult and fabulous sciences, and believed in the existence of phenomena impossible in the moral as well as in the physical order of things. They believed that through me they possessed the philosopher's stone, the universal panacea, the intercourse with all the elementary, heavenly, and infernal spirits; they had no doubt whatever that, thanks to my sublime science, they could find out the secrets of every government in Europe.

After they had assured themselves of the reality of my cabalistic science by questions respecting the past, they decided to turn it to some use by consulting it upon the present and upon the future. I had no difficulty in skewing myself a good guesser, because I always gave answers with a double meaning, one of the meanings being carefully arranged by me, so as not to be understood until after the event; in that manner, my cabalistic science, like the oracle of Delphi, could never be found in fault. I saw how easy it must have been for the ancient heathen priests to impose upon ignorant, and therefore credulous mankind. I saw how easy it will always be for impostors to find dupes, and I realized, even better than the Roman orator, why two augurs could never look at each other without laughing; it was because they had both an equal interest in giving importance to the deceit they perpetrated, and from which they derived such immense profits. But what I could not, and probably never shall, understand, was the reason for which the Fathers, who were not so simple or so ignorant as our Evangelists, did not feel able to deny the divinity of oracles, and, in order to get out of the difficulty, ascribed them to the devil. They never would have entertained such a strange idea if they had been acquainted with cabalistic science. My three worthy friends were like the holy Fathers; they had intelligence and wit, but they were superstitious, and no philosophers. But, although believing fully in my oracles, they were too kind-hearted to think them the work of the devil, and it suited their natural goodness better to believe my answers inspired by some heavenly spirit. They were not only good Christians and faithful to the Church, but even real devotees and full of scruples. They were not married, and, after having renounced all commerce with women, they had become the enemies of the female sex; perhaps a strong proof of the weakness of their minds. They imagined that chastity was the condition 'sine qua non' exacted by the spirits from those who wished to have intimate communication or intercourse with them: they fancied that spirits excluded women, and 'vice versa'.

With all these oddities, the three friends were truly intelligent and even witty, and, at the beginning of my acquaintance with them, I could not reconcile these antagonistic points. But a prejudiced mind cannot reason well, and the faculty of reasoning is the most important of all. I often laughed when I heard them talk on religious matters; they would ridicule those whose intellectual faculties were so limited that they could not understand the mysteries of religion. The incarnation of the Word, they would say, was a trifle for God, and therefore easy to understand,

and the resurrection was so comprehensible that it did not appear to them wonderful, because, as God cannot die, Jesus Christ was naturally certain to rise again. As for the Eucharist, transubstantiation, the real presence, it was all no mystery to them, but palpable evidence, and yet they were not Jesuits. They were in the habit of going to confession every week, without feeling the slightest trouble about their confessors, whose ignorance they kindly regretted. They thought themselves bound to confess only what was a sin in their own opinion, and in that, at least, they reasoned with good sense.

With those three extraordinary characters, worthy of esteem and respect for their moral qualities, their honesty, their reputation, and their age, as well as for their noble birth, I spent my days in a very pleasant manner: although, in their thirst for knowledge, they often kept me hard at work for ten hours running, all four of us being locked up together in a room, and unapproachable to everybody, even to friends or relatives.

I completed the conquest of their friendship by relating to them the whole of my life, only with some proper reserve, so as not to lead them into any capital sins. I confess candidly that I deceived them, as the Papa Deldimopulo used to deceive the Greeks who applied to him for the oracles of the Virgin. I certainly did not act towards them with a true sense of honesty, but if the reader to whom I confess myself is acquainted with the world and with the spirit of society, I entreat him to think before judging me, and perhaps I may meet with some indulgence at his hands.

I might be told that if I had wished to follow the rules of pure morality I ought either to have declined intimate intercourse with them or to have undeceived them. I cannot deny these premises, but I will answer that I was only twenty years of age, I was intelligent, talented, and had just been a poor fiddler. I should have lost my time in trying to cure them of their weakness; I should not have succeeded, for they would have laughed in my face, deplored my ignorance, and the result of it all would have been my dismissal. Besides, I had no mission, no right, to constitute myself an apostle, and if I had heroically resolved on leaving them as soon as I knew them to be foolish visionaries, I should have shewn myself a misanthrope, the enemy of those worthy men for whom I could procure innocent pleasures, and my own enemy at the same time; because, as a young man, I liked to live well, to enjoy all the pleasures natural to youth and to a good constitution.

By acting in that manner I should have failed in common politeness, I should perhaps have caused or allowed M. de Bragadin's death, and I should have exposed those three honest men to becoming the victims of the first bold cheat who, ministering to their monomania, might have won their favour, and would have ruined them by inducing them to undertake the chemical operations of the Great Work. There is also another consideration, dear reader, and as I love you I will tell you what it is. An invincible self-love would have prevented me from declaring myself unworthy of their friendship either by my ignorance or by my pride; and I should have been guilty of great rudeness if I had ceased to visit them.

I took, at least it seems to me so, the best, the most natural, and the noblest decision, if we consider the disposition of their mind, when I decided upon the plan of conduct which insured me the necessaries of life and of those necessaries who could be a better judge than your very humble servant?

Through the friendship of those three men, I was certain of obtaining consideration and influence in my own country. Besides, I found it very flattering to my vanity to become the subject of the speculative chattering of empty fools who, having nothing else to do, are always trying to find out the cause of every moral phenomenon they meet with, which their narrow intellect cannot understand.

People racked their brain in Venice to find out how my intimacy with three men of that high character could possibly exist; they were wrapped up in heavenly aspirations, I was a world's devotee; they were very strict in their morals, I was thirsty of all pleasures! At the beginning of summer, M. de Bragadin was once, more able to take his seat in the senate, and, the day before he went out for the first time, he spoke to me thus:

"Whoever you may be, I am indebted to you for my life. Your first protectors wanted to make you a priest, a doctor, an advocate, a soldier, and ended by making a fiddler of you; those persons did not know you. God had evidently instructed your guardian angel to bring you to me. I know you and appreciate you. If you will be my son, you have only to acknowledge me for your father, and, for the future, until my death, I will treat you as my own child. Your apartment is ready, you may send your clothes: you shall have a servant, a gondola at your orders, my own table, and ten sequins a month. It is the sum I used to receive from my father when I was your age. You need not think of the future; think only of enjoying yourself, and take me as your adviser in everything that may happen to you, in everything you may wish to undertake, and you may be certain of always finding me your friend."

I threw myself at his feet to assure him of my gratitude, and embraced him calling him my father. He folded me in his arms, called me his dear son; I promised to love and to obey him; his two friends, who lived in the same palace, embraced me affectionately, and we swore eternal fraternity.

Such is the history of my metamorphosis, and of the lucky stroke which, taking me from the vile profession of a fiddler, raised me to the rank of a grandee.

III

Fortune, which had taken pleasure in giving me a specimen of its despotic caprice, and had insured my happiness through means which sages would disavow, had not the power to make me adopt a system of moderation and prudence which alone could establish my future welfare on a firm basis.

My ardent nature, my irresistible love of pleasure, my unconquerable independence, would not allow me to submit to the reserve which my new position in life demanded from me. I began to lead a life of complete freedom, caring for nothing but what ministered to my tastes, and I thought that, as long as I respected the laws, I could trample all prejudices under my feet. I fancied that I could live free and independent in a country ruled entirely by an aristocratic government, but this was not the case, and would not have been so even if fortune had raised me to a seat in that same government, for the Republic of Venice, considering that its primary duty is to preserve its own integrity, finds itself the slave of its own policy, and is bound to sacrifice everything to self-preservation, before which the laws themselves cease to be inviolable.

But let us abandon the discussion of a principle now too trite, for humankind, at least in Europe, is satisfied that unlimited liberty is nowhere consistent with a properly-regulated state of society. I have touched lightly on the matter, only to give to my readers some idea of my conduct in my own country, where I began to tread a path which was to lead me to a state prison as inscrutable as it was unconstitutional.

With enough money, endowed by nature with a pleasing and commanding physical appearance, a confirmed gambler, a true spendthrift, a great talker, very far from modest, intrepid, always running after pretty women, supplanting my rivals, and acknowledging no good company but that which ministered to my enjoyment, I was certain to be disliked; but, ever ready to expose myself to any danger, and to take the responsibility of all my actions, I thought I had a right to do anything I pleased, for I always broke down abruptly every obstacle I found in my way.

Such conduct could not but be disagreeable to the three worthy men whose oracle I had become, but they did not like to complain. The excellent M. de Bragadin would only tell me that I was giving him a repetition of the foolish life he had himself led at my age, but that I must prepare to pay the penalty of my follies, and to feel the punishment when I should reach his time of life. Without wanting in the respect I owed him, I would turn his terrible forebodings into jest, and continue my course of extravagance. However, I must mention here the first proof he gave me of his true wisdom.

At the house of Madame Avogadro, a woman full of wit in spite of her sixty years, I had made the acquaintance of a young Polish nobleman called Zawoiski. He was expecting money from Poland, but in the mean time the Venetian ladies did not let him want for any, being all very much in love with his handsome face and his Polish manners. We soon became good friends, my purse was his, but, twenty years later, he assisted me to a far greater extent in Munich. Zawoiski was honest, he had only a small dose of intelligence, but it was enough for his happiness. He died in Trieste five or six years ago, the ambassador of the Elector of Treves. I will speak of him in another part of these Memoirs.

This amiable young man, who was a favourite with everybody and was thought a free-thinker because he frequented the society of Angelo Querini and Lunardo Venier, presented me one day, as we were out walking, to an unknown countess who took my fancy very strongly. We called on her in the evening, and, after introducing me to her husband, Count Rinaldi, she invited us to remain and have supper.

The count made a faro bank in the course of the evening, I punted with his wife as a partner, and won some fifty ducats.

Very much pleased with my new acquaintance, I called alone on the countess the next morning. The count, apologizing for his wife who was not up yet, took me to her room. She received me with graceful ease, and, her husband having left us alone, she had the art to let me hope for every favour, yet without committing herself; when I took leave of her, she invited me to supper for the evening. After supper I played, still in partnership with her, won again, and went away very much in love. I did not fail to pay her another visit the next morning, but when I presented myself at the house I was told that she had gone out.

I called again in the evening, and, after she had excused herself for not having been at home in the morning, the faro bank began, and I lost all my money, still having the countess for my partner. After supper, and when the other guests had retired, I remained with Zawoiski, Count Rinaldi having offered to give us our revenge. As I had no more money, I played upon trust, and the count threw down the cards after I had lost five hundred sequins. I went away in great sorrow. I was bound in honour to pay the next morning, and I did not possess a groat. Love increased my despair, for I saw myself on the point of losing the esteem of a woman by whom I was smitten, and the anxiety I felt did not escape M. de Bragadin when we met in the morning. He kindly encouraged me to confess my troubles to him. I was conscious that it was my only chance, and candidly related the whole affair, and I ended by saying that I should not survive my disgrace. He consoled me by promising that my debt would be cancelled in the course of the day, if I would swear never to play again upon trust. I took an oath to that effect, and kissing his hand, I went out for a walk, relieved from a great load. I had no doubt that my excellent father would give me five hundred sequins during the day, and I enjoyed my anticipation the honour I would derive, in the opinion of the lovely countess, by my exactitude and prompt discharge of my debt. I felt that it gave new strength to my hopes, and that feeling prevented me from regretting my heavy loss, but grateful for the great generosity of my benefactor I was fully determined on keeping my promise.

I dined with the three friends, and the matter was not even alluded to; but, as we were rising from the table, a servant brought M. de Bragadin a letter and a parcel.

He read the letter, asked me to follow him into his study, and the moment we were alone, he said;

"Here is a parcel for you."

I opened it, and found some forty sequins. Seeing my surprise, M. de Bragadin laughed merrily and handed me the letter, the contents of which ran thus:

> M. de Casanova may be sure that our playing last night was
> only a joke: he owes me nothing. My wife begs to send him
> half of the gold which he has lost in cash.
>
> Count Rinaldi

I looked at M. de Bragadin, perfectly amazed, and he burst out laughing. I guessed the truth, thanked him, and embracing him tenderly I promised to be wiser for the future. The mist I had before my eyes was dispelled, I felt that my love was defunct, and I remained rather ashamed, when I realized that I had been the dupe of the wife as well as of the husband.

"This evening," said my clever physician, "you can have a gay supper with the charming countess."

"This evening, my dear, respected benefactor, I will have supper with you. You have given me a masterly lesson."

"The next time you lose money upon trust, you had better not pay it."

"But I should be dishonoured."

"Never mind. The sooner you dishonour yourself, the more you will save, for you will always be compelled to accept your dishonour whenever you find yourself utterly unable to pay your losses. It is therefore more prudent not to wait until then."

"It is much better still to avoid that fatal impossibility by never playing otherwise than with money in hand."

"No doubt of it, for then you will save both your honour and your purse. But, as you are fond of games of chance, I advise you never to punt. Make the bank, and the advantage must be on your side."

"Yes, but only a slight advantage."

"As slight as you please, but it will be on your side, and when the game is over you will find yourself a winner and not a loser. The punter is excited, the banker is calm. The last says, 'I bet you do not guess,' while the first says, 'I bet I can guess.' Which is the fool, and which is the wise man? The question is easily answered. I adjure you to be prudent, but if you should punt and win, recollect that you are only an idiot if at the end you lose."

"Why an idiot? Fortune is very fickle."

"It must necessarily be so; it is a natural consequence. Leave off playing, believe me, the very moment you see luck turning, even if you should, at that moment, win but one groat."

I had read Plato, and I was astonished at finding a man who could reason like Socrates.

The next day, Zawoiski called on me very early to tell me that I had been expected to supper, and that Count Rinaldi had praised my promptness in paying my debts of honour. I did not think it necessary to undeceive him, but I did not go again to Count Rinaldi's, whom I saw sixteen years afterwards in Milan. As to Zawoiski, I did not tell him the story till I met him in Carlsbad, old and deaf, forty years later.

Three or four months later, M. de Bragadin taught me another of his masterly lessons. I had become acquainted, through Zawoiski, with a Frenchman called L'Abbadie, who was then soliciting from the Venetian Government the appointment of inspector of the armies of the Republic. The senate appointed, and I presented him to my protector, who promised him his vote; but the circumstance I am going to relate prevented him from fulfilling his promise.

I was in need of one hundred sequins to discharge a few debts, and I begged M. de Bragadin to give them to me.

"Why, my dear son, do you not ask M. de l'Abbadie to render you that service?"

"I should not dare to do so, dear father."

"Try him; I am certain that he will be glad to lend you that sum."

"I doubt it, but I will try."

I called upon L'Abbadie on the following day, and after a short exchange of compliments I told him the service I expected from his friendship. He excused himself in a very polite manner, drowning his refusal in that sea of commonplaces which people are sure to repeat when they cannot or will not oblige a friend. Zawoiski came in as he was still apologizing, and I left them together. I hurried at once to M. de Bragadin, and told him my want of success. He merely remarked that the Frenchman was deficient in intelligence.

It just happened that it was the very day on which the appointment of the inspectorship was to be brought before the senate. I went out to attend to my business (I ought to say to my pleasure), and as I did not return home till after midnight I went to bed without seeing my father. In the morning I said in his presence that I intended to call upon L'Abbadie to congratulate him upon his appointment.

"You may spare yourself that trouble; the senate has rejected his nomination."

"How so? Three days ago L'Abbadie felt sure of his success."

"He was right then, for he would have been appointed if I had not made up my mind to speak against him. I have proved to the senate that a right policy forbade the government to trust such an important post to a foreigner."

"I am much surprised, for your excellency was not of that opinion the day before yesterday."

"Very true, but then I did not know M. de l'Abbadie. I found out only yesterday that the man was not sufficiently intelligent to fill the position he was soliciting. Is he likely to possess a sane judgment when he refuses to lend you one hundred sequins? That refusal has cost him an important appointment and an income of three thousand crowns, which would now be his."

When I was taking my walk on the same day I met Zawoiski with L'Abbadie, and did not try to avoid them. L'Abbadie was furious, and he had some reason to be so.

"If you had told me," he said angrily, "that the one hundred sequins were intended as a gag to stop M. de Bragadin's mouth, I would have contrived to procure them for you."

"If you had had an inspector's brains you would have easily guessed it."

The Frenchman's resentment proved very useful to me, because he related the circumstance to everybody. The result was that from that time those who wanted the patronage of the senator applied to me. Comment is needless; this sort of thing has long been in existence, and will long remain so, because very often, to obtain the highest of favours, all that is necessary is to obtain the good-will of a minister's favourite or even of his valet. My debts were soon paid.

It was about that time that my brother Jean came to Venice with Guarienti, a converted Jew, a great judge of paintings, who was travelling at the expense of His Majesty the King of Poland, and Elector of Saxony. It was the converted Jew who had purchased for His Majesty the gallery of the Duke of Modena for one hundred thousand sequins. Guarienti and my brother left Venice for Rome, where Jean remained in the studio of the celebrated painter Raphael Mengs, whom we shall meet again hereafter.

Now, as a faithful historian, I must give my readers the story of a certain adventure in which were involved the honour and happiness of one of the most charming women in Italy, who would have been unhappy if I had not been a thoughtless fellow.

In the early part of October, 1746, the theatres being opened, I was walking about with my mask on when I perceived a woman, whose head was well enveloped in the hood of her mantle, getting out of the Ferrara barge which had just arrived. Seeing her alone, and observing her uncertain walk, I felt myself drawn towards her as if an unseen hand had guided me.

I come up to her, and offer my services if I can be of any use to her. She answers timidly that she only wants to make some enquiries.

"We are not here in the right place for conversation," I say to her; "but if you would be kind enough to come with me to a cafe, you would be able to speak and to explain your wishes."

She hesitates, I insist, and she gives way. The tavern was close at hand; we go in, and are alone in a private room. I take off my mask, and out of politeness she must put down the hood of her mantle. A large muslin head-dress conceals half of her face, but her eyes, her nose, and her pretty mouth are enough to let me see on her features beauty, nobleness, sorrow, and that candour which gives youth such an undefinable charm. I need not say that, with such a good letter of introduction, the unknown at once captivated my warmest interest. After wiping away a few tears which are flowing, in spite of all her efforts, she tells me that she belongs to a noble family, that she has run away from her father's house, alone, trusting in God, to meet a Venetian nobleman who had seduced her and then deceived her, thus sealing her everlasting misery.

"You have then some hope of recalling him to the path of duty? I suppose he has promised you marriage?"

"He has engaged his faith to me in writing. The only favour I claim from your kindness is to take me to his house, to leave me there, and to keep my secret."

"You may trust, madam, to the feelings of a man of honour. I am worthy of your trust. Have entire confidence in me, for I already take a deep interest in all your concerns. Tell me his name."

"Alas! sir, I give way to fate."

With these words, she takes out of her bosom a paper which she gives me; I recognize the handwriting of Zanetto Steffani. It was a promise of marriage by which he engaged his word of honour to marry within a week, in Venice, the young countess A—— S——. When I have read the paper, I return it to her, saying that I knew the writer quite well, that he was connected with the chancellor's office, known as a great libertine, and deeply in debt, but that he would be rich after his mother's death.

"For God's sake take me to his house."

"I will do anything you wish; but have entire confidence in me, and be good enough to hear me. I advise you not to go to his house. He has already done you great injury, and, even supposing that you should happen to find him at home, he might be capable of receiving you badly; if he should not be at home, it is most likely that his mother would not exactly welcome you, if you should tell her who you are and what is your errand. Trust to me, and be quite certain that God has sent me on your way to assist you. I promise you that to-morrow at the latest you shall know whether Steffani is in Venice, what he intends to do with you, and what we may compel him to do. Until then my advice is not to let him know your arrival in Venice."

"Good God! where shall I go to-night?"

"To a respectable house, of course."

"I will go to yours, if you are married."

"I am a bachelor."

I knew an honest widow who resided in a lane, and who had two furnished rooms. I persuade the young countess to follow me, and we take a gondola. As we are gliding along, she tells me that, one month before, Steffani had stopped in her neighbourhood for necessary repairs to his travelling-carriage, and that, on the same day he had made her acquaintance at a house where she had gone with her mother for the purpose of offering their congratulations to a newly-married lady.

"I was unfortunate enough," she continued, "to inspire him with love, and he postponed his departure. He remained one month in C——, never going out but in the evening, and spending every night under my windows conversing with me. He swore a thousand times that he adored me, that his intentions were honourable. I entreated him to present himself to my parents to ask me in marriage, but he always excused himself by alleging some reason, good or bad, assuring me that he could not be happy unless I shewed him entire confidence. He would beg of me to make up my mind to run away with him, unknown to everybody, promising that my honour should not suffer from such a step, because, three days after my departure, everybody should receive notice of my being his wife, and he assured me that he would bring me back on a visit to my native place shortly after our marriage. Alas! sir! what shall I say now? Love blinded me; I fell into the abyss; I believed him; I agreed to everything. He gave me the paper which you have read, and the following night I allowed him to come into my room through the window under which he was in the habit of conversing with me.

"I consented to be guilty of a crime which I believed would be atoned for within three days, and he left me, promising that the next night he would be again under my window, ready to receive me in his arms. Could I possibly entertain any doubt after the fearful crime I had committed for him? I prepared a small parcel, and waited for his coming, but in vain. Oh! what a cruel long night it was! In the morning I heard that the monster had gone away with his servant one hour after sealing my shame. You may imagine my despair! I adopted the only plan that despair could suggest, and that, of course, was not the right one. One hour before midnight I left my father's roof, alone, thus completing my dishonour, but resolved on death, if the man who has cruelly robbed me of my most precious treasure, and whom a natural instinct told me I could find here, does not restore me the honour which he alone can give me back. I walked all night and nearly the whole day, without taking any food, until I got into the barge, which brought me here in twenty-four hours. I travelled in the boat with five men and two women, but no one saw my face or heard my voice, I kept constantly sitting down in a corner, holding my head down, half asleep, and with this prayer-book in my hands. I was left alone, no one spoke to me, and I thanked God for it. When I landed on the wharf, you did not give me time to think how I could find out the dwelling of my perfidious seducer, but you may imagine the impression produced upon me by the sudden apparition of a masked man who, abruptly, and as if placed there purposely by Providence, offered me his services; it seemed to me that you had guessed my distress, and, far from experiencing any repugnance, I felt that I was acting rightly in trusting myself in your hands, in spite of all prudence which, perhaps, ought to have made me turn a deaf ear to your words, and refuse the invitation to enter alone with you the house to which you took me.

"You know all now, sir; but I entreat you not to judge me too severely; I have been virtuous all through my life; one month ago I had never committed a fault which could call a blush upon my face, and the bitter tears which I shed every day will, I hope, wash out my crime in the eyes of God. I have been carefully brought up, but love and the want of experience have thrown me into the abyss. I am in your hands, and I feel certain that I shall have no cause to repent it."

I needed all she had just told' me to confirm me in the interest which I had felt in her from the first moment. I told her unsparingly that Steffani had seduced and abandoned her of malice aforethought, and that she ought to think of him only to be revenged of his perfidy. My words made her shudder, and she buried her beautiful face in her hands.

We reached the widow's house. I established her in a pretty, comfortable room, and ordered some supper for her, desiring the good landlady to skew her every attention and to let her want for nothing. I then took an affectionate leave of her, promising to see her early in the morning.

On leaving this interesting but hapless girl, I proceeded to the house of Steffani. I heard from one of his mother's gondoliers that he had returned to Venice three days before, but that, twenty-four hours after his return, he had gone away again without any servant, and nobody knew his whereabouts, not even his mother. The same evening, happening to be seated next to an abbe from Bologna at the theatre, I asked him several questions respecting the family of my unfortunate protegee.

The abbe being intimately acquainted with them, I gathered from him all the information I required, and, amongst other things, I heard that the young countess had a brother, then an officer in the papal service.

Very early the next morning I called upon her. She was still asleep. The widow told me that she had made a pretty good supper, but without speaking a single word, and that she had locked herself up in her room immediately afterwards. As soon as she had opened her door, I entered her room, and, cutting short her apologies for having kept me waiting, I informed her of all I had heard.

Her features bore the stamp of deep sorrow, but she looked calmer, and her complexion was no longer pale. She thought it unlikely that Steffani would have left for any other place but for C——. Admitting the possibility that she might be right, I immediately offered to go to C—— myself, and to return without loss of time to fetch her, in case Steffani should be there. Without giving her time to answer I told her all the particulars I had learned concerning her honourable family, which caused her real satisfaction.

"I have no objection," she said, "to your going to C——, and I thank you for the generosity of your offer, but I beg you will postpone your journey. I still hope that Steffani will return, and then I can take a decision."

"I think you are quite right," I said. "Will you allow me to have some breakfast with you?"

"Do you suppose I could refuse you?"

"I should be very sorry to disturb you in any way. How did you use to amuse yourself at home?"

"I am very fond of books and music; my harpsichord was my delight."

I left her after breakfast, and in the evening I came back with a basket full of good books and music, and I sent her an excellent harpsichord. My kindness confused her, but I surprised her much more when I took out of my pocket three pairs of slippers. She blushed, and thanked me with great feeling. She had walked a long distance, her shoes were evidently worn out, her feet sore, and she appreciated the delicacy of my present. As I had no improper design with regard to her, I enjoyed her gratitude, and felt pleased at the idea she evidently entertained of my kind attentions. I had no other purpose in view but to restore calm to her mind, and to obliterate the bad opinion which the unworthy Steffani had given her of men in general. I never thought of inspiring her with love for me, and I had not the slightest idea that I could fall in love with her. She was unhappy, and her unhappiness—a sacred thing in my eyes—called all the more for my most honourable sympathy, because, without knowing me, she had given me her entire confidence. Situated as she was, I could not suppose her heart susceptible of harbouring a new affection, and I would have despised myself if I had tried to seduce her by any means in my power.

I remained with her only a quarter of an hour, being unwilling that my presence should trouble her at such a moment, as she seemed to be at a loss how to thank me and to express all her gratitude.

I was thus engaged in a rather delicate adventure, the end of which I could not possibly foresee, but my warmth for my protegee did not cool down, and having no difficulty in procuring the means to keep her I had no wish to see the last scene of the romance. That singular meeting, which gave me the useful opportunity of finding myself endowed with generous dispositions, stronger even than my love for pleasure, flattered my self-love more than I could express. I was then trying a great experiment, and conscious that I wanted sadly to study myself, I gave up all my energies to acquire the great science of the 'xxxxxxxxxxxx'.

On the third day, in the midst of expressions of gratitude which I could not succeed in stopping she told me that she could not conceive why I shewed her so much sympathy, because I ought to have formed but a poor opinion of her in consequence of the readiness with which she had followed me into the cafe. She smiled when I answered that I could not understand how I had succeeded in giving her so great a confidence in my virtue, when I appeared before her with a mask on my face, in a costume which did not indicate a very virtuous character.

"It was easy for me, madam," I continued, "to guess that you were a beauty in distress, when I observed your youth, the nobleness of your countenance, and, more than all, your candour. The stamp of truth was so well affixed to the first words you uttered that I could not have the shadow of a doubt left in me as to your being the unhappy victim of the most natural of all feelings, and as to your having abandoned your home through a sentiment of honour. Your fault was that of a warm heart seduced by love, over which reason could have no sway, and your flight—the action of a soul crying for reparation or for revenge-fully justifies you. Your cowardly seducer must pay with his life the penalty due to his crime, and he ought never to receive, by marrying you, an unjust reward, for he is not worthy of possessing you after degrading himself by the vilest conduct."

"Everything you say is true. My brother, I hope, will avenge me."

"You are greatly mistaken if you imagine that Steffani will fight your brother; Steffani is a coward who will never expose himself to an honourable death."

As I was speaking, she put her hand in her pocket and drew forth, after a few moments' consideration, a stiletto six inches long, which she placed on the table.

"What is this?" I exclaimed.

"It is a weapon upon which I reckoned until now to use against myself in case I should not succeed in obtaining reparation for the crime I have committed. But you have opened my eyes. Take away, I entreat you, this stiletto, which henceforth is useless to me. I trust in your friendship, and I have an inward certainty that I shall be indebted to you for my honour as well as for my life."

I was struck by the words she had just uttered, and I felt that those words, as well as her looks, had found their way to my heart, besides enlisting my generous sympathy. I took the stiletto, and left her with so much agitation that I had to acknowledge the weakness of my heroism, which I was very near turning into ridicule; yet I had the wonderful strength to perform, at least by halves, the character of a Cato until the seventh day.

I must explain how a certain suspicion of the young lady arose in my mind. That doubt was heavy on my heart, for, if it had proved true, I should have been a dupe, and the idea was humiliating. She had told me that she was a musician; I had immediately sent her a harpsichord, and, yet, although the instrument had been at her disposal for three days, she had not opened it once, for the widow had told me so. It seemed to me that the best way to thank me for my attentive kindness would have been to give me a specimen of her musical talent. Had she deceived me? If so, she would lose my esteem. But, unwilling to form a hasty judgment, I kept on my guard, with a firm determination to make good use of the first opportunity that might present itself to clear up my doubts.

I called upon her the next day after dinner, which was not my usual time, having resolved on creating the opportunity myself. I caught her seated before a toilet-glass, while the widow dressed the most beautiful auburn hair I had ever seen. I tendered my apologies for my sudden appearance at an unusual hour; she excused herself for not having completed her toilet, and the widow went on with her work. It was the first time I had seen the whole of her face, her neck, and half of her arms, which the graces themselves had moulded. I remained in silent contemplation. I praised, quite by chance, the perfume of the pomatum, and the widow took the opportunity of telling her that she had spent in combs, powder, and pomatum the three livres she had received from her. I recollected then that she had told me the first day that she had left C—— with ten paoli.

I blushed for very shame, for I ought to have thought of that.

As soon as the widow had dressed her hair, she left the room to prepare some coffee for us. I took up a ring which had been laid by her on the toilet-table, and I saw that it contained a portrait exactly like her; I was amused at the singular fancy she had had of having her likeness taken in a man's costume, with black hair. "You are mistaken," she said, "it is a portrait of my brother. He is two years older than I, and is an officer in the papal army."

I begged her permission to put the ring on her finger; she consented, and when I tried, out of mere gallantry, to kiss her hand, she drew it back, blushing. I feared she might be offended, and I assured her of my respect.

"Ah, sir!" she answered, "in the situation in which I am placed, I must think of defending myself against my own self much more than against you."

The compliment struck me as so fine, and so complimentary to me, that I thought it better not to take it up, but she could easily read in my eyes that she would never find me ungrateful for whatever feelings she might entertain in my favour. Yet I felt my love taking such proportions that I did not know how to keep it a mystery any longer.

Soon after that, as she was again thanking me for the books—I had given her, saying that I had guessed her taste exactly, because she did not like novels, she added, "I owe you an apology for not having sung to you yet, knowing that you are fond of music." These words made me breathe freely; without waiting for any answer, she sat down before the instrument and played several pieces with a facility, with a precision, with an expression of which no words could convey any idea. I was in ecstacy. I entreated her to sing; after some little ceremony, she took one of the music books I had given her, and she sang at sight in a manner which fairly ravished me. I begged that she would allow me to kiss her hand, and she did not say yes, but when I took it and pressed my lips on it, she did not oppose any resistance; I had the courage to smother my ardent desires, and the kiss I imprinted on her lovely hand was a mixture of tenderness, respect, and admiration.

I took leave of her, smitten, full of love, and almost determined on declaring my passion. Reserve becomes silliness when we know that our affection is returned by the woman we love, but as yet I was not quite sure.

The disappearance of Steffani was the talk of Venice, but I did not inform the charming countess of that circumstance. It was generally supposed that his mother had refused to pay his debts, and that he had run away to avoid his creditors. It was very possible. But, whether he returned or not, I could not make up my mind to lose the precious treasure I had in my hands. Yet I did not see in what manner, in what quality, I could enjoy that treasure, and I found myself in a regular maze. Sometimes I had an idea of consulting my kind father, but I would soon abandon it with fear, for I had made a trial of his empiric treatment in the Rinaldi affair, and still more in the case of l'Abbadie. His remedies frightened me to that extent that I would rather remain ill than be cured by their means.

One morning I was foolish enough to enquire from the widow whether the lady had asked her who I was. What an egregious blunder! I saw it when the good woman, instead of answering me, said,

"Does she not know who you are?"

"Answer me, and do not ask questions," I said, in order to hide my confusion.

The worthy woman was right; through my stupidity she would now feel curious; the tittle-tattle of the neighbourhood would of course take up the affair and discuss it; and all through my thoughtlessness!

It was an unpardonable blunder. One ought never to be more careful than in addressing questions to half-educated persons. During the fortnight that she had passed under my protection, the countess had shewn me no curiosity whatever to know anything about me, but it did not prove that she was not curious on the subject. If I had been wise, I should have told her the very first day who I was, but I made up for my mistake that evening better than anybody else could have done it, and, after having told her all about myself, I entreated her forgiveness for not having done so sooner. Thanking me for my confidence, she confessed how curious she had been to know me better, and she assured me that she would never have been imprudent enough to ask any questions about me from her landlady. Women have a more delicate, a surer tact than men, and her last words were a home-thrust for me.

Our conversation having turned to the extraordinary absence of Steffani, she said that her father must necessarily believe her to be hiding with him somewhere. "He must have found out," she added, "that I was in the habit of conversing with him every night from my window, and he must have heard of my having embarked for Venice on board the Ferrara barge. I feel certain that my father is now in Venice, making secretly every effort to discover me. When he visits this city he always puts up at Boncousin; will you ascertain whether he is there?"

She never pronounced Steffani's name without disgust and hatred, and she said she would bury herself in a convent, far away from her native place, where no one could be acquainted with her shameful history.

I intended to make some enquiries the next day, but it was not necessary for me to do so, for in the evening, at supper-time, M. Barbaro said to us,

"A nobleman, a subject of the Pope, has been recommended to me, and wishes me to assist him with my influence in a rather delicate and intricate matter. One of our citizens has, it appears, carried off his daughter, and has been hiding somewhere with her for the last fortnight, but nobody knows where. The affair ought to be brought before the Council of Ten, but the mother of the ravisher claims to be a relative of mine, and I do not intend to interfere."

I pretended to take no interest in M. Barbaro's words, and early the next morning I went to the young countess to tell her the interesting news. She was still asleep; but, being in a hurry, I sent the widow to say that I wanted to see her only for two minutes in order to communicate something of great importance. She received me, covering herself up to the chin with the bed-clothes.

As soon as I had informed her of all I knew, she entreated me to enlist M. Barbaro as a mediator between herself and her father, assuring me that she would rather die than become the wife of the monster who had dishonoured her. I undertook to do it, and she gave me the promise of marriage used by the deceiver to seduce her, so that it could be shewn to her father.

In order to obtain M. Barbaro's mediation in favour of the young countess, it would have been necessary to tell him that she was under my protection, and I felt it would injure my protegee. I took no determination at first, and most likely one of the reasons for my hesitation was that I saw myself on the point of losing her, which was particularly repugnant to my feelings.

After dinner Count A—— S—— was announced as wishing to see M. Barbaro. He came in with his son, the living portrait of his sister. M. Barbaro took them to his study to talk the matter over, and within an hour they had taken leave. As soon as they had gone, the excellent M. Barbaro asked me, as I had expected, to consult my heavenly spirit, and to ascertain whether he would be right in interfering in favour of Count A——S——. He wrote the question himself, and I gave the following answer with the utmost coolness:

"You ought to interfere, but only to advise the father to forgive his daughter and to give up all idea of compelling her to marry her ravisher, for Steffani has been sentenced to death by the will of God."

The answer seemed wonderful to the three friends, and I was myself surprised at my boldness, but I had a foreboding that Steffani was to meet his death at the hands of somebody; love might have given birth to that presentiment. M. de Bragadin, who believed my oracle infallible, observed that it had never given such a clear answer, and that Steffani was certainly dead. He said to M. de Barbaro,

"You had better invite the count and his son to dinner hereto-morrow. You must act slowly and prudently; it would be necessary to know where the daughter is before you endeavour to make the father forgive her."

M. Barbaro very nearly made me drop my serious countenance by telling me that if I would try my oracle I could let them know at once where the girl was. I answered that I would certainly ask my spirit on the morrow, thus gaining time in order to ascertain before hand the disposition of the father and of his son. But I could not help laughing, for I had placed myself under the necessity of sending Steffani to the next world, if the reputation of my oracle was to be maintained.

I spent the evening with the young countess, who entertained no doubt either of her father's indulgence or of the entire confidence she could repose in me.

What delight the charming girl experienced when she heard that I would dine the next day with her father and brother, and that I would tell her every word that would be said about her! But what happiness it was for me to see her convinced that she was right in loving me, and that, without me, she would certainly have been lost in a town where the policy of the government tolerates debauchery as a solitary species of individual freedom. We congratulated each other upon our fortuitous meeting and upon the conformity in our tastes, which we thought truly wonderful. We were greatly pleased that her easy acceptance of my invitation, or my promptness in persuading her to follow and to trust me, could not be ascribed to the mutual attraction of our features, for I was masked, and her hood was then as good as a mask. We entertained no doubt that everything had been arranged by Heaven to get us acquainted, and to fire us both, even unknown to ourselves, with love for each other.

"Confess," I said to her, in a moment of enthusiasm, and as I was covering her hand with kisses, "confess that if you found me to be in love with you you would fear me."

"Alas! my only fear is to lose you."

That confession, the truth of which was made evident by her voice and by her looks, proved the electric spark which ignited the latent fire. Folding her rapidly in my arms, pressing my mouth on her lips, reading in her beautiful eyes neither a proud indignation nor the cold compliance which might have been the result of a fear of losing me, I gave way entirely to the sweet inclination of love, and swimming already in a sea of delights I felt my enjoyment increased a hundredfold when I saw, on the countenance of the beloved creature who shared it, the expression of happiness, of love, of modesty, and of sensibility, which enhances the charm of the greatest triumph.

She had scarcely recovered her composure when she cast her eyes down and sighed deeply. Thinking that I knew the cause of it, I threw myself on my knees before her, and speaking to her words of the warmest affection I begged, I entreated her, to forgive me.

"What offence have I to forgive you for, dear friend? You have not rightly interpreted my thoughts. Your love caused me to think of my happiness, and in that moment a cruel recollection drew that sigh from me. Pray rise from your knees."

Midnight had struck already; I told her that her good fame made it necessary for me to go away; I put my mask on and left the house. I was so surprised, so amazed at having obtained a felicity of which I did not think myself worthy, that my departure must have appeared rather abrupt to her. I could not sleep. I passed one of those disturbed nights during which the imagination of an amorous young man is unceasingly running after the shadows of reality. I had tasted, but not savoured, that happy reality, and all my being was longing for her who alone could make my enjoyment complete. In that nocturnal drama love and imagination were the two principal actors; hope, in the background, performed only a dumb part. People may say what they please on that subject but hope is in fact nothing but a deceitful flatterer accepted by reason only because it is often in need of palliatives. Happy are those men who, to enjoy life to the fullest extent, require neither hope nor foresight.

In the morning, recollecting the sentence of death which I had passed on Steffani, I felt somewhat embarrassed about it. I wished I could have recalled it, as well for the honour of my oracle, which was seriously implicated by it, as for the sake of Steffani himself, whom I did not hate half so much since I was indebted to him for the treasure in my possession.

The count and his son came to dinner. The father was simple, artless, and unceremonious. It was easy to read on his countenance the grief he felt at the unpleasant adventure of his daughter, and his anxiety to settle the affair honourably, but no anger could be traced on his features or in his manners. The son, as handsome as the god of love, had wit and great nobility of manner. His easy, unaffected carriage pleased me, and wishing to win his friendship I shewed him every attention.

After the dessert, M. Barbaro contrived to persuade the count that we were four persons with but one head and one heart, and the worthy nobleman spoke to us without any reserve. He praised his daughter very highly. He assured us that Steffani had never entered his house, and therefore he could not conceive by what spell, speaking to his daughter only at night and from the street under the window, he had succeeded in seducing her to such an extent as to make her leave her home alone, on foot, two days after he had left himself in his post-chaise.

"Then," observed M. Barbaro, "it is impossible to be certain that he actually seduced her, or to prove that she went off with him."

"Very true, sir, but although it cannot be proved, there is no doubt of it, and now that no one knows where Steffani is, he can be nowhere but with her. I only want him to marry her."

"It strikes me that it would be better not to insist upon a compulsory marriage which would seal your daughter's misery, for Steffani is, in every respect, one of the most worthless young men we have amongst our government clerks."

"Were I in your place," said M. de Bragadin, "I would let my daughter's repentance disarm my anger, and I would forgive her."

"Where is she? I am ready to fold her in my arms, but how can I believe in her repentance when it is evident that she is still with him."

"Is it quite certain that in leaving C—— she proceeded to this city?"

"I have it from the master of the barge himself, and she landed within twenty yards of the Roman gate. An individual wearing a mask was waiting for her, joined her at once, and they both disappeared without leaving any trace of their whereabouts."

"Very likely it was Steffani waiting there for her."

"No, for he is short, and the man with the mask was tall. Besides, I have heard that Steffani had left Venice two days before the arrival of my daughter. The man must have been some friend of Steffani, and he has taken her to him."

"But, my dear count, all this is mere supposition."

"There are four persons who have seen the man with the mask, and pretend to know him, only they do not agree. Here is a list of four names, and I will accuse these four persons before the Council of Ten, if Steffani should deny having my daughter in his possession."

The list, which he handed to M. Barbaro, gave not only the names of the four accused persons, but likewise those of their accusers. The last name, which M. Barbaro read, was mine. When I heard it, I shrugged my shoulders in a manner which caused the three friends to laugh heartily.

M. de Bragadin, seeing the surprise of the count at such uncalled-for mirth, said to him,

"This is Casanova my son, and I give you my word of honour that, if your daughter is in his hands, she is perfectly safe, although he may not look exactly the sort of man to whom young girls should be trusted."

The surprise, the amazement, and the perplexity of the count and his son were an amusing picture. The loving father begged me to excuse him, with tears in his eyes, telling me to place myself in his position. My only answer was to embrace him most affectionately.

The man who had recognized me was a noted pimp whom I had thrashed some time before for having deceived me. If I had not been there just in time to take care of the young countess, she would not have escaped him, and he would have ruined her for ever by taking her to some house of ill-fame.

The result of the meeting was that the count agreed to postpone his application to the Council of Ten until Steffani's place of refuge should be discovered.

"I have not seen Steffani for six months, sir," I said to the count, "but I promise you to kill him in a duel as soon as he returns."

"You shall not do it," answered the young count, very coolly, "unless he kills me first."

"Gentlemen," exclaimed M. de Bragadin, "I can assure you that you will neither of you fight a duel with him, for Steffani is dead."

"Dead!" said the count.

"We must not," observed the prudent Barbaro, "take that word in its literal sense, but the wretched man is dead to all honour and self-respect."

After that truly dramatic scene, during which I could guess that the denouement of the play was near at hand, I went to my charming countess, taking care to change my gondola three times—a necessary precaution to baffle spies.

I gave my anxious mistress an exact account of all the conversation. She was very impatient for my coming, and wept tears of joy when I repeated her father's words of forgiveness; but when I told her that nobody knew of Steffani having entered her chamber, she fell on her knees and thanked God. I then repeated her brother's words, imitating his coolness: "You shall not kill him, unless he kills me first." She kissed me tenderly, calling me her guardian angel, her saviour, and weeping in my arms. I promised to bring her brother on the following day, or the day after that at the latest. We had our supper, but we did not talk of Steffani, or of revenge, and after that pleasant meal we devoted two hours to the worship of the god of love.

I left her at midnight, promising to return early in the morning—my reason for not remaining all night with her was that the landlady might, if necessary, swear without scruple that I had never spent a night with the young girl. It proved a very lucky inspiration of mine, for, when I arrived home, I found the three friends waiting impatiently for me in order to impart to me wonderful news which M. de Bragadin had heard at the sitting of the senate.

"Steffani," said M. de Bragadin to me, "is dead, as our angel Paralis revealed it to us; he is dead to the world, for he has become a Capuchin friar. The senate, as a matter of course, has been informed of it. We alone are aware that it is a punishment which God has visited upon him. Let us worship the Author of all things, and the heavenly hierarchy which renders us worthy of knowing what remains a mystery to all men. Now we must achieve our undertaking, and console the poor father. We must enquire from Paralis where the girl is. She cannot now be with Steffani. Of course, God has not condemned her to become a Capuchin nun."

"I need not consult my angel, dearest father, for it is by his express orders that I have been compelled until now to make a mystery of the refuge found by the young countess."

I related the whole story, except what they had no business to know, for, in the opinion of the worthy men, who had paid heavy tribute to Love, all intrigues were fearful crimes. M. Dandolo and M. Barbaro expressed their surprise when they heard that the young girl had been under my protection for a fortnight, but M. de Bragadin said that he was not astonished, that it was according to cabalistic science, and that he knew it.

"We must only," he added, "keep up the mystery of his daughter's place of refuge for the count, until we know for a certainty that he will forgive her, and that he will take her with him to C——, or to any other place where he may wish to live hereafter."

"He cannot refuse to forgive her," I said, "when he finds that the amiable girl would never have left C—— if her seducer had not given her this promise of marriage in his own handwriting. She walked as far as the barge, and she landed at the very moment I was passing the Roman gate. An inspiration from above told me to accost her and to invite her to follow me. She obeyed, as if she was fulfilling the decree of Heaven, I took her to a refuge impossible to discover, and placed her under the care of a God-fearing woman."

My three friends listened to me so attentively that they looked like three statues. I advised them to invite the count to dinner for the day after next, because I needed some time to consult 'Paralis de modo tenendi'. I then told M. Barbaro to let the count know in what sense he was to understand Steffani's death. He undertook to do it, and we retired to rest.

I slept only four or five hours, and, dressing myself quickly, hurried to my beloved mistress. I told the widow not to serve the coffee until we called for it, because we wanted to remain quiet and undisturbed for some hours, having several important letters to write.

I found the lovely countess in bed, but awake, and her eyes beaming with happiness and contentment. For a fortnight I had only seen her sad, melancholy, and thoughtful. Her pleased countenance, which I naturally ascribed to my influence, filled me with joy. We commenced as all happy lovers always do, and we were both unsparing of the mutual proofs of our love, tenderness, and gratitude.

After our delightful amorous sport, I told her the news, but love had so completely taken possession of her pure and sensitive soul, that what had been important was now only an accessory. But the news of her seducer having turned a Capuchin friar filled her with amazement, and, passing very sensible remarks on the extraordinary event, she pitied Steffani. When we can feel pity, we love no longer, but a feeling of pity succeeding love is the characteristic only of a great and generous mind. She was much pleased with me for having informed my three friends of her being under my protection, and she left to my care all the necessary arrangements for obtaining a reconciliation with her father.

Now and then we recollected that the time of our separation was near at hand, our grief was bitter, but we contrived to forget it in the ecstacy of our amorous enjoyment.

"Ah! why can we not belong for ever to each other?" the charming girl would exclaim. "It is not my acquaintance with Steffani, it is your loss which will seal my eternal misery."

But it was necessary to bring our delightful interview to a close, for the hours were flying with fearful rapidity. I left her happy, her eyes wet with tears of intense felicity.

At the dinner-table M. Barbaro told me that he had paid a visit to his relative, Steffani's mother, and that she had not appeared sorry at the decision taken by her son, although he was her only child.

"He had the choice," she said, "between killing himself and turning friar, and he took the wiser course."

The woman spoke like a good Christian, and she professed to be one; but she spoke like an unfeeling mother, and she was truly one, for she was wealthy, and if she had not been cruelly avaricious her son would not have been reduced to the fearful alternative of committing suicide or of becoming a Capuchin friar.

The last and most serious motive which caused the despair of Steffani, who is still alive, remained a mystery for everybody. My Memoirs will raise the veil when no one will care anything about it.

The count and his son were, of course, greatly surprised, and the event made them still more desirous of discovering the young lady. In order to obtain a clue to her place of refuge, the count had resolved on summoning before the Council of Ten all the parties, accused and accusing, whose names he had on his list, with the exception of myself. His determination made it necessary for us to inform him that his daughter was in my hands, and M. de Bragadin undertook to let him know the truth.

We were all invited to supper by the count, and we went to his hostelry, with the exception of M. de Bragadin, who had declined the invitation. I was thus prevented from seeing my divinity that evening, but early the next morning I made up for lost time, and as it had been decided that her father would on that very day be informed of her being under my care, we remained together until noon. We had no hope of contriving another meeting, for I had promised to bring her brother in the afternoon.

The count and his son dined with us, and after dinner M. de Bragadin said,

"I have joyful news for you, count; your beloved daughter has been found!"

What an agreeable surprise for the father and son! M. de Bragadin handed them the promise of marriage written by Steffani, and said,

"This, gentlemen, evidently brought your lovely young lady to the verge of madness when she found that he had gone from C—— without her. She left your house alone on foot, and as she landed in Venice Providence threw her in the way of this young man, who induced her to follow him, and has placed her under the care of an honest woman, whom she has not left since, whom she will leave only to fall in your arms as soon as she is certain of your forgiveness for the folly she has committed."

"Oh! let her have no doubt of my forgiving her," exclaimed the father, in the ecstacy of joy, and turning to me, "Dear sir, I beg of you not to delay the fortunate moment on which the whole happiness of my life depends."

I embraced him warmly, saying that his daughter would be restored to him on the following day, and that I would let his son see her that very afternoon, so as to give him an opportunity of preparing her by degrees for that happy reconciliation. M. Barbaro desired to accompany us, and the young man, approving all my arrangements, embraced me, swearing everlasting friendship and gratitude.

We went out all three together, and a gondola carried us in a few minutes to the place where I was guarding a treasure more precious than the golden apples of the Hesperides. But, alas! I was on the point of losing that treasure, the remembrance of which causes me, even now, a delicious trembling.

I preceded my two companions in order to prepare my lovely young friend for the visit, and when I told her that, according to my arrangements, her father would not see her till on the following day:

"Ah!" she exclaimed with the accent of true happiness, "then we can spend a few more hours together! Go, dearest, go and bring my brother."

I returned with my companions, but how can I paint that truly dramatic situation? Oh! how inferior art must ever be to nature! The fraternal love, the delight beaming upon those two beautiful faces, with a slight shade of confusion on that of the sister, the pure joy shining in the midst of their tender caresses, the most eloquent exclamations followed by a still more eloquent silence, their loving looks which seem like flashes of lightning in the midst of a dew of tears, a thought of politeness which brings blushes on her countenance, when she recollects that she has forgotten her duty towards a nobleman whom she sees for the first time, and finally there was my part, not a speaking one, but yet the most important of all. The whole formed a living picture to which the most skilful painter could not have rendered full justice.

We sat down at last, the young countess between her brother and M. Barbaro, on the sofa, I, opposite to her, on a low foot-stool.

"To whom, dear sister, are we indebted for the happiness of having found you again?"

"To my guardian angel," she answered, giving me her hand, "to this generous man who was waiting for me, as if Heaven had sent him with the special mission of watching over your sister; it is he who has saved me, who has prevented me from falling into the gulf which yawned under my feet, who has rescued me from the shame threatening me, of which I had then no conception; it is to him I am indebted for all, to him who, as you see, kisses my hand now for the first time."

And she pressed her handkerchief to her beautiful eyes to dry her tears, but ours were flowing at the same time.

Such is true virtue, which never loses its nobleness, even when modesty compels it to utter some innocent falsehood. But the charming girl had no idea of being guilty of an untruth. It was a pure, virtuous soul which was then speaking through her lips, and she allowed it to speak. Her virtue seemed to whisper to her that, in spite of her errors, it had never deserted her. A young girl who gives way to a real feeling of love cannot be guilty of a crime, or be exposed to remorse.

Towards the end of our friendly visit, she said that she longed to throw herself at her father's feet, but that she wished to see him only in the evening, so as not to give any opportunity to the gossips of the place, and it was agreed that the meeting, which was to be the last scene of the drama, should take place the next day towards the evening.

We returned to the count's hostelry for supper, and the excellent man, fully persuaded that he was indebted to me for his honour as well as for his daughter's, looked at me with admiration, and spoke to me with gratitude. Yet he was not sorry to have ascertained himself, and before I had said so, that I had been the first man who had spoken to her after landing. Before parting in the evening, M. Barbaro invited them to dinner for the next day.

I went to my charming mistress very early the following morning, and, although there was some danger in protracting our interview, we did not give it a thought, or, if we did, it only caused us to make good use of the short time that we could still devote to love.

After having enjoyed, until our strength was almost expiring, the most delightful, the most intense voluptuousness in which mutual ardour can enfold two young, vigorous, and passionate lovers, the young countess dressed herself, and, kissing her slippers, said she would never part with them as long as she lived. I asked her to give me a lock of her hair, which she did at once. I meant to have it made into a chain like the one woven with the hair of Madame F——, which I still wore round my neck.

Towards dusk, the count and his son, M. Dandolo, M. Barbaro, and myself, proceeded together to the abode of the young countess. The moment she saw her father, she threw herself on her knees before him, but the count, bursting into tears, took her in his arms, covered her with kisses, and breathed over her words of forgiveness, of love and blessing. What a scene for a man of sensibility! An hour later we escorted the family to the inn, and, after wishing them a pleasant journey, I went back with my two friends to M. de Bragadin, to whom I gave a faithful account of what had taken place.

We thought that they had left Venice, but the next morning they called at the place in a peotta with six rowers. The count said that they could not leave the city without seeing us once more; without thanking us again, and me particularly, for all we had done for them. M. de Bragadin, who had not seen the young countess before, was struck by her extraordinary likeness to her brother.

They partook of some refreshments, and embarked in their peotta, which was to carry them, in twenty-four hours, to Ponte di Lago Oscuro, on the River Po, near the frontiers of the papal states. It was only with my eyes that I could express to the lovely girl all the feelings which filled my heart, but she understood the language, and I had no difficulty in interpreting the meaning of her looks.

Never did an introduction occur in better season than that of the count to M. Barbaro. It saved the honour of a respectable family; and it saved me from the unpleasant consequences of an interrogatory in the presence of the Council of Ten, during which I should have been convicted of having taken the young girl with me, and compelled to say what I had done with her.

A few days afterwards we all proceeded to Padua to remain in that city until the end of autumn. I was grieved not to find Doctor Gozzi in Padua; he had been appointed to a benefice in the country, and he was living there with Bettina; she had not been able to remain with the scoundrel who had married her only for the sake of her small dowry, and had treated her very ill.

I did not like the quiet life of Padua, and to avoid dying from ennui I fell in love with a celebrated Venetian courtesan. Her name was Ancilla; sometime after, the well-known dancer, Campioni, married her and took her to London, where she caused the death of a very worthy Englishman. I shall have to mention her again in four years; now I have only to speak of a certain circumstance which brought my love adventure with her to a close after three or four weeks.

Count Medini, a young, thoughtless fellow like myself, and with inclinations of much the same cast, had introduced me to Ancilla. The count was a confirmed gambler and a thorough enemy of fortune. There was a good deal of gambling going on at Ancilla's, whose favourite lover he was, and the fellow had presented me to his mistress only to give her the opportunity of making a dupe of me at the card-table.

And, to tell the truth, I was a dupe at first; not thinking of any foul play, I accepted ill luck without complaining; but one day I caught them cheating. I took a pistol out of my pocket, and, aiming at Medini's breast, I threatened to kill him on the spot unless he refunded at once all the gold they had won from me. Ancilla fainted away, and the count, after refunding the money, challenged me to follow him out and measure swords. I placed my pistols on the table, and we went out. Reaching a convenient spot, we fought by the bright light of the moon, and I was fortunate enough to give him a gash across the shoulder. He could not move his arm, and he had to cry for mercy.

After that meeting, I went to bed and slept quietly, but in the morning I related the whole affair to my father, and he advised me to leave Padua immediately, which I did.

Count Medini remained my enemy through all his life. I shall have occasion to speak of him again when I reach Naples.

The remainder of the year 1746 passed off quietly, without any events of importance. Fortune was now favourable to me and now adverse.

Towards the end of January, 1747, I received a letter from the young countess A—— S——, who had married the Marquis of——. She entreated me not to appear to know her, if by chance I visited the town in which she resided, for she had the happiness of having linked her destiny to that of a man who had won her heart after he had obtained her hand.

I had already heard from her brother that, after their return to C——, her mother had taken her to the city from which her letter was written, and there, in the house of a relative with whom she was residing, she had made the acquaintance of the man who had taken upon himself the charge of her future welfare and happiness. I saw her one year afterwards, and if it had not been for her letter, I should certainly have solicited an introduction to her husband. Yet, peace of mind has greater charms even than love; but, when love is in the way, we do not think so.

For a fortnight I was the lover of a young Venetian girl, very handsome, whom her father, a certain Ramon, exposed to public admiration as a dancer at the theatre. I might have remained longer her captive, if marriage had not forcibly broken my chains. Her protectress, Madame Cecilia Valmarano, found her a very proper husband in the person of a French dancer, called Binet, who had assumed the name of Binetti, and thus his young wife had not to become a French woman; she soon won great fame in more ways than one. She was strangely privileged; time with its heavy hand seemed to have no power over her. She always appeared young, even in the eyes of the best judges of faded, bygone female beauty. Men, as a general rule, do not ask for anything more, and they are right in not racking their brain for the sake of being convinced that they are the dupes of external appearance. The last lover that the wonderful Binetti killed by excess of amorous enjoyment was a certain Mosciuski, a Pole, whom fate brought to Venice seven or eight years ago; she had then reached her sixty-third year!

My life in Venice would have been pleasant and happy, if I could have abstained from punting at basset. The ridotti were only open to noblemen who had to appear without masks, in their patrician robes, and wearing the immense wig which had become indispensable since the beginning of the century. I would play, and I was wrong, for I had neither prudence enough to leave off when fortune was adverse, nor sufficient control over myself to stop when I had won. I was then gambling through a feeling of avarice. I was extravagant by taste, and I always regretted the money I had spent, unless it had been won at the gaming-table, for it was only in that case that the money had, in my opinion, cost me nothing.

At the end of January, finding myself under the necessity of procuring two hundred sequins, Madame Manzoni contrived to obtain for me from another woman the loan of a diamond ring worth five hundred. I made up my mind to go to Treviso, fifteen miles distant from Venice, to pawn the ring at the Mont-de-piete, which there lends money upon valuables at the rate of five per cent. That useful establishment does not exist in Venice, where the Jews have always managed to keep the monopoly in their hands.

I got up early one morning, and walked to the end of the canale regio, intending to engage a gondola to take me as far as Mestra, where I could take post horses, reach Treviso in less than two hours, pledge my diamond ring, and return to Venice the same evening.

As I passed along St. Job's Quay, I saw in a two-oared gondola a country girl beautifully dressed. I stopped to look at her; the gondoliers, supposing that I wanted an opportunity of reaching Mestra at a cheap rate, rowed back to the shore.

Observing the lovely face of the young girl, I do not hesitate, but jump into the gondola, and pay double fare, on condition that no more passengers are taken. An elderly priest was seated near the young girl, he rises to let me take his place, but I politely insist upon his keeping it.

IV

I Fall in Love with Christine, and Find a Husband Worthy of Her—Christine's Wedding

T hose gondoliers," said the elderly priest, ad dressing me in order to begin the conversation, "are very fortunate. They took us up at the Rialto for thirty soldi, on condition that they would be allowed to embark other passengers, and here is one already; they will certainly find more."

"When I am in a gondola, reverend sir, there is no room left for any more passengers."

So saying, I give forty more soldi to the gondoliers, who, highly pleased with my generosity, thank me and call me excellency. The good priest, accepting that title as truly belonging to me, entreats my pardon for not having addressed me as such.

"I am not a Venetian nobleman, reverend sir, and I have no right to the title of Excellenza."

"Ah!" says the young lady, "I am very glad of it."

"Why so, signora?"

"Because when I find myself near a nobleman I am afraid. But I suppose that you are an illustrissimo."

"Not even that, signora; I am only an advocate's clerk."

"So much the better, for I like to be in the company of persons who do not think themselves above me. My father was a farmer, brother of my uncle here, rector of P——, where I was born and bred. As I am an only daughter I inherited my father's property after his death, and I shall likewise be heiress to my mother, who has been ill a long time and cannot live much longer, which causes me a great deal of sorrow; but it is the doctor who says it. Now, to return to my subject, I do not suppose that there is much difference between an advocate's clerk and the daughter of a rich farmer. I only say so for the sake of saying something, for I know very well that, in travelling, one must accept all sorts of companions: is it not so, uncle?"

"Yes, my dear Christine, and as a proof you see that this gentleman has accepted our company without knowing who or what we are."

"But do you think I would have come if I had not been attracted by the beauty of your lovely niece?"

At these words the good people burst out laughing. As I did not think that there was anything very comic in what I had said, I judged that my travelling companions were rather simple, and I was not sorry to find them so.

"Why do you laugh so heartily, beautiful 'demigella'? Is it to shew me your fine teeth? I confess that I have never seen such a splendid set in Venice."

"Oh! it is not for that, sir, although everyone in Venice has paid me the same compliment. I can assure you that in P—— all the 'girls have teeth as fine as mine. Is it not a fact, uncle?"

"Yes, my dear niece."

"I was laughing, sir, at a thing which I will never tell you."

"Oh! tell me, I entreat you."

"Oh! certainly not, never."

"I will tell you myself," says the curate.

"You will not," she exclaims, knitting her beautiful eyebrows. "If you do I will go away."

"I defy you to do it, my dear. Do you know what she said, sir, when she saw you on the wharf? 'Here is a very handsome young man who is looking at me, and would not be sorry to be with us.' And when she saw that the gondoliers were putting back for you to embark she was delighted."

While the uncle was speaking to me, the indignant niece was slapping him on the shoulder.

"Why are you angry, lovely Christine, at my hearing that you liked my appearance, when I am so glad to let you know how truly charming I think you?"

"You are glad for a moment. Oh! I know the Venetians thoroughly now. They have all told me that they were charmed with me, and not one of those I would have liked ever made a declaration to me."

"What sort of declaration did you want?"

"There's only one sort for me, sir; the declaration leading to a good marriage in church, in the sight of all men. Yet we remained a fortnight in Venice; did we not, uncle?"

"This girl," said the uncle, "is a good match, for she possesses three thousand crowns. She has always said that she would marry only a Venetian, and I have accompanied her to Venice to give her an opportunity of being known. A worthy woman gave us hospitality for a fortnight, and has presented my niece in several houses where she made the acquaintance of marriageable young men, but those who pleased her would not hear of marriage, and those who would have been glad to marry her did not take her fancy."

"But do you imagine, reverend sir, that marriages can be made like omelets? A fortnight in Venice, that is nothing; you ought to live there at least six months. Now, for instance, I think your niece sweetly pretty, and I should consider myself fortunate if the wife whom God intends for me were like her, but, even if she offered me now a dowry of fifty thousand crowns on condition that our wedding takes place immediately, I would refuse her. A prudent young man wants to know the character of a girl before he marries her, for it is neither money nor beauty which can ensure happiness in married life."

"What do you mean by character?" asked Christine; "is it a beautiful hand-writing?"

"No, my dear. I mean the qualities of the mind and the heart. I shall most likely get married sometime, and I have been looking for a wife for the last three years, but I am still looking in vain. I have known several young girls almost as lovely as you are, and all with a good marriage portion, but after an acquaintance of two or three months I found out that they could not make me happy."

"In what were they deficient?"

"Well, I will tell you, because you are not acquainted with them, and there can be no indiscretion on my part. One whom I certainly would have married, for I loved her dearly, was extremely vain. She would have ruined me in fashionable clothes and by her love for luxuries. Fancy! she was in the habit of paying one sequin every month to the hair-dresser, and as much at least for pomatum and perfumes."

"She was a giddy, foolish girl. Now, I spend only ten soldi in one year on wax which I mix with goat's grease, and there I have an excellent pomatum."

"Another, whom I would have married two years ago, laboured under a disease which would have made me unhappy; as soon as I knew of it, I ceased my visits."

"What disease was it?"

"A disease which would have prevented her from being a mother, and, if I get married, I wish to have children."

"All that is in God's hands, but I know that my health is excellent. Is it not, uncle?"

"Another was too devout, and that does not suit me. She was so over-scrupulous that she was in the habit of going to her confessor twice a week, and every time her confession lasted at least one hour. I want my wife to be a good Christian, but not bigoted."

"She must have been a great sinner, or else she was very foolish. I confess only once a month, and get through everything in two minutes. Is it not true, uncle? and if you were to ask me any questions, uncle, I should not know what more to say."

"One young lady thought herself more learned than I, although she would, every minute, utter some absurdity. Another was always low-spirited, and my wife must be cheerful."

"Hark to that, uncle! You and my mother are always chiding me for my cheerfulness."

"Another, whom I did not court long, was always afraid of being alone with me, and if I gave her a kiss she would run and tell her mother."

"How silly she must have been! I have never yet listened to a lover, for we have only rude peasants in P——, but I know very well that there are some things which I would not tell my mother."

"One had a rank breath; another painted her face, and, indeed, almost every young girl is guilty of that fault. I am afraid marriage is out of the question for me, because I want, for instance, my wife to have black eyes, and in our days almost every woman colours them by art; but I cannot be deceived, for I am a good judge."

"Are mine black?"

"You are laughing?"

"I laugh because your eyes certainly appear to be black, but they are not so in reality. Never mind, you are very charming in spite of that."

"Now, that is amusing. You pretend to be a good judge, yet you say that my eyes are dyed black. My eyes, sir, whether beautiful or ugly, are now the same as God made them. Is it not so, uncle?"

"I never had any doubt of it, my dear niece."

"And you do not believe me, sir?"

"No, they are too beautiful for me to believe them natural."

"Oh, dear me! I cannot bear it."

"Excuse me, my lovely damigella, I am afraid I have been too sincere."

After that quarrel we remained silent. The good curate smiled now and then, but his niece found it very hard to keep down her sorrow.

At intervals I stole a look at her face, and could see that she was very near crying. I felt sorry, for she was a charming girl. In her hair, dressed in the fashion of wealthy countrywomen, she had more than one hundred sequins' worth of gold pins and arrows which fastened the plaits of her long locks as dark as ebony. Heavy gold ear-rings, and a long chain, which was wound twenty times round her snowy neck, made a fine contrast to her complexion, on which the lilies and the roses were admirably blended. It was the first time that I had seen a country beauty in such splendid apparel. Six years before, Lucie at Pasean had captivated me, but in a different manner.

Christine did not utter a single word, she was in despair, for her eyes were truly of the greatest beauty, and I was cruel enough to attack them. She evidently hated me, and her anger alone kept back her tears. Yet I would not undeceive her, for I wanted her to bring matters to a climax.

When the gondola had entered the long canal of Marghera, I asked the clergyman whether he had a carriage to go to Treviso, through which place he had to pass to reach P——.

"I intended to walk," said the worthy man, "for my parish is poor and I am the same, but I will try to obtain a place for Christine in some carriage travelling that way."

"You would confer a real kindness on me if you would both accept a seat in my chaise; it holds four persons, and there is plenty of room."

"It is a good fortune which we were far from expecting"

"Not at all, uncle; I will not go with this gentleman."

"Why not, my dear niece?"

"Because I will not."

"Such is the way," I remarked, without looking at her, "that sincerity is generally rewarded."

"Sincerity, sir! nothing of the sort," she exclaimed, angrily, "it is sheer wickedness. There can be no true black eyes now for you in the world, but, as you like them, I am very glad of it."

"You are mistaken, lovely Christine, for I have the means of ascertaining the truth."

"What means?"

"Only to wash the eyes with a little lukewarm rose-water; or if the lady cries, the artificial colour is certain to be washed off."

At those words, the scene changed as if by the wand of a conjuror. The face of the charming girl, which had expressed nothing but indignation, spite and disdain, took an air of contentment and of placidity delightful to witness. She smiled at her uncle who was much pleased with the change in her countenance, for the offer of the carriage had gone to his heart.

"Now you had better cry a little, my dear niece, and 'il signore' will render full justice to your eyes."

Christine cried in reality, but it was immoderate laughter that made her tears flow.

That species of natural originality pleased me greatly, and as we were going up the steps at the landing-place, I offered her my full apologies; she accepted the carriage. I ordered breakfast, and told a 'vetturino' to get a very handsome chaise ready while we had our meal, but the curate said that he must first of all go and say his mass.

"Very well, reverend sir, we will hear it, and you must say it for my intention."

I put a silver ducat in his hand.

"It is what I am in the habit of giving," I observed.

My generosity surprised him so much that he wanted to kiss my hand. We proceeded towards the church, and I offered my arm to the niece who, not knowing whether she ought to accept it or not, said to me,

"Do you suppose that I cannot walk alone?"

"I have no such idea, but if I do not give you my arm, people will think me wanting in politeness."

"Well, I will take it. But now that I have your arm, what will people think?"

"Perhaps that we love each other and that we make a very nice couple."

"And if anyone should inform your mistress that we are in love with each other, or even that you have given your arm to a young girl?"

"I have no mistress, and I shall have none in future, because I could not find a girl as pretty as you in all Venice."

"I am very sorry for you, for we cannot go again to Venice; and even if we could, how could we remain there six months? You said that six months were necessary to know a girl well."

"I would willingly defray all your expenses."

"Indeed? Then say so to my uncle, and he will think it over, for I could not go alone."

"In six months you would know me likewise."

"Oh! I know-you very well already."

"Could you accept a man like me?"

"Why not?"

"And will you love me?"

"Yes, very much, when you are my husband."

I looked at the young girl with astonishment. She seemed to me a princess in the disguise of a peasant girl. Her dress, made of 'gros de Tours' and all embroidered in gold, was very handsome, and cost certainly twice as much as the finest dress of a Venetian lady. Her bracelets, matching the neckchain, completed her rich toilet. She had the figure of a nymph, and the new fashion of wearing a mantle not having yet reached her village, I could see the most magnificent bosom, although her dress was fastened up to the neck. The end of the richly-embroidered skirt did not go lower than the ankles, which allowed me to admire the neatest little foot and the lower part of an exquisitely moulded leg. Her firm and easy walk, the natural freedom of all her movements, a charming look which seemed to say, "I am very glad that you think me pretty," everything, in short, caused the ardent fire of amorous desires to circulate through my veins. I could not conceive how such a lovely girl could have spent a fortnight in Venice without finding a man to marry or to deceive her. I was particularly delighted with her simple, artless way of talking, which in the city might have been taken for silliness.

Absorbed in my thoughts, and having resolved in my own mind on rendering brilliant homage to her charms, I waited impatiently for the end of the mass.

After breakfast I had great difficulty in convincing the curate that my seat in the carriage was the last one, but I found it easier to persuade him on our arrival in Treviso to remain for dinner and for supper at a small, unfrequented inn, as I took all the expense upon myself. He accepted very willingly when I added that immediately after supper a carriage would be in readiness to convey him to P——, where he would arrive in an hour after a peasant journey by moonlight. He had nothing to hurry him on, except his wish to say mass in his own church the next morning.

I ordered a fire and a good dinner, and the idea struck me that the curate himself might pledge the ring for me, and thus give me the opportunity of a short interview with his niece. I proposed it to him, saying that I could not very well go myself, as I did not wish to be known. He undertook the commission at once, expressing his pleasure at doing something to oblige me.

He left us, and I remained alone with Christine. I spent an hour with her without trying to give her even a kiss, although I was dying to do so, but I prepared her heart to burn with the same desires which were already burning in me by those words which so easily inflame the imagination of a young 'girl.

The curate came back and returned me the ring, saying that it could not be pledged until the day after the morrow, in consequence of the Festival of the Holy Virgin. He had spoken to the cashier, who had stated that if I liked the bank would lend double the sum I had asked.

"My dear sir," I said, "you would greatly oblige me if you would come back here from P—— to pledge the ring yourself. Now that it has been offered once by you, it might look very strange if it were brought by another person. Of course I will pay all your expenses."

"I promise you to come back."

I hoped he would bring his niece with him.

I was seated opposite to Christine during the dinner, and discovered fresh charms in her every minute, but, fearing I might lose her confidence if I tried to obtain some slight favour, I made up my mind not to go to work too quickly, and to contrive that the curate should take her again to Venice. I thought that there only I could manage to bring love into play and to give it the food it requires.

"Reverend sir," I said, "let me advise you to take your niece again to Venice. I undertake to defray all expenses, and to find an honest woman with whom your Christine will be as safe as with her own mother. I want to know her well in order to make her my wife, and if she comes to Venice our marriage is certain."

"Sir, I will bring my niece myself to Venice as soon as you inform me that you have found a worthy woman with whom I can leave her in safety."

While we were talking I kept looking at Christine, and I could see her smile with contentment.

"My dear Christine," I said, "within a week I shall have arranged the affair. In the meantime, I will write to you. I hope that you have no objection to correspond with me."

"My uncle will write for me, for I have never been taught writing."

"What, my dear child! you wish to become the wife of a Venetian, and you cannot write."

"Is it then necessary to know how to write in order to become a wife? I can read well."

"That is not enough, and although a girl can be a wife and a mother without knowing how to trace one letter, it is generally admitted that a young girl ought to be able to write. I wonder you never learned."

"There is no wonder in that, for not one girl in our village can do it. Ask my uncle."

"It is perfectly true, but there is not one who thinks of getting married in Venice, and as you wish for a Venetian husband you must learn."

"Certainly," I said, "and before you come to Venice, for everybody would laugh at you, if you could not write. I see that it makes you sad, my dear, but it cannot be helped."

"I am sad, because I cannot learn writing in a week."

"I undertake," said her uncle, "to teach you in a fortnight, if you will only practice diligently. You will then know enough to be able to improve by your own exertions."

"It is a great undertaking, but I accept it; I promise you to work night and day, and to begin to-morrow."

After dinner, I advised the priest not to leave that evening, to rest during the night, and I observed that, by going away before day-break, he would reach P—— in good time, and feel all the better for it. I made the same proposal to him in the evening, and when he saw that his niece was sleepy, he was easily persuaded to remain. I called for the innkeeper, ordered a carriage for the clergyman, and desired that a fire might be lit for me in the next room where I would sleep, but the good priest said that it was unnecessary, because there were two large beds in our room, that one would be for me and the other for him and his niece.

"We need not undress," he added, "as we mean to leave very early, but you can take off your clothes, sir, because you are not going with us, and you will like to remain in bed to-morrow morning."

"Oh!" remarked Christine, "I must undress myself, otherwise I could not sleep, but I only want a few minutes to get ready in the morning."

I said nothing, but I was amazed. Christine then, lovely and charming enough to wreck the chastity of a Xenocrates, would sleep naked with her uncle! True, he was old, devout, and without any of the ideas which might render such a position dangerous, yet the priest was a man, he had evidently felt like all men, and he ought to have known the danger he was exposing himself to. My carnal-mindedness could not realize such a state of innocence. But it was truly innocent, so much so that he did it openly, and did not suppose that anyone could see anything wrong in it. I saw it all plainly, but I was not accustomed to such things, and felt lost in wonderment. As I advanced in age and in experience, I have seen the same custom established in many countries amongst honest people whose good morals were in no way debased by it, but it was amongst good people, and I do not pretend to belong to that worthy class.

We had had no meat for dinner, and my delicate palate was not over-satisfied. I went down to the kitchen myself, and I told the landlady that I wanted the best that could be procured in Treviso for supper, particularly in wines.

"If you do not mind the expense, sir, trust to me, and I undertake to please you. I will give you some Gatta wine."

"All right, but let us have supper early."

When I returned to our room, I found Christine caressing the cheeks of her old uncle, who was laughing; the good man was seventy-five years old.

"Do you know what is the matter?" he said to me; "my niece is caressing me because she wants me to leave her here until my return. She tells me that you were like brother and sister during the hour you have spent alone together this morning, and I believe it, but she does not consider that she would be a great trouble to you."

"Not at all, quite the reverse, she will afford me great pleasure, for I think her very charming. As to our mutual behaviour, I believe you can trust us both to do our duty."

"I have no doubt of it. Well, I will leave her under your care until the day after to-morrow. I will come back early in the morning so as to attend to your business."

This extraordinary and unexpected arrangement caused the blood to rush to my head with such violence that my nose bled profusely for a quarter of an hour. It did not frighten me, because I was used to such accidents, but the good priest was in a great fright, thinking that it was a serious haemorrhage.

When I had allayed his anxiety, he left us on some business of his own, saying that he would return at night-fall. I remained alone with the charming, artless Christine, and lost no time in thanking her for the confidence she placed in me.

"I can assure you," she said, "that I wish you to have a thorough knowledge of me; you will see that I have none of the faults which have displeased you so much in the young ladies you have known in Venice, and I promise to learn writing immediately."

"You are charming and true; but you must be discreet in P——, and confide to no one that we have entered into an agreement with each other. You must act according to your uncle's instructions, for it is to him that I intend to write to make all arrangements."

"You may rely upon my discretion. I will not say anything even to my mother, until you give me permission to do so."

I passed the afternoon, in denying myself even the slightest liberties with my lovely companion, but falling every minute deeper in love with her. I told her a few love stories which I veiled sufficiently not to shock her modesty. She felt interested, and I could see that, although she did not always understand, she pretended to do so, in order not to appear ignorant.

When her uncle returned, I had arranged everything in my mind to make her my wife, and I resolved on placing her, during her stay in Venice, in the house of the same honest widow with whom I had found a lodging for my beautiful Countess A—— S——.

We had a delicious supper. I had to teach Christine how to eat oysters and truffles, which she then saw for the first time. Gatta wine is like champagne, it causes merriment without intoxicating, but it cannot be kept for more than one year. We went to bed before midnight, and it was broad daylight when I awoke. The curate had left the room so quietly that I had not heard him.

I looked towards the other bed, Christine was asleep. I wished her good morning, she opened her eyes, and leaning on her elbow, she smiled sweetly.

"My uncle has gone. I did not hear him."

"Dearest Christine, you are as lovely as one of God's angels. I have a great longing to give you a kiss."

"If you long for a kiss, my dear friend, come and give me one."

I jump out of my bed, decency makes her hide her face. It was cold, and I was in love. I find myself in her arms by one of those spontaneous movements which sentiment alone can cause, and we belong to each other without having thought of it, she happy and rather confused, I delighted, yet unable to realize the truth of a victory won without any contest.

An hour passed in the midst of happiness, during which we forgot the whole world. Calm followed the stormy gusts of passionate love, and we gazed at each other without speaking.

Christine was the first to break the silence

"What have we done?" she said, softly and lovingly.

"We have become husband and wife."

"What will my uncle say to-morrow?"

"He need not know anything about it until he gives us the nuptial benediction in his own church."

"And when will he do so?"

"As soon as we have completed all the arrangements necessary for a public marriage."

"How long will that be?"

"About a month."

"We cannot be married during Lent."

"I will obtain permission."

"You are not deceiving me?"

"No, for I adore you."

"Then, you no longer want to know me better?"

"No; I know you thoroughly now, and I feel certain that you will make me happy."

"And will you make me happy, too?"

"I hope so."

"Let us get up and go to church. Who could have believed that, to get a husband, it was necessary not to go to Venice, but to come back from that city!"

We got up, and, after partaking of some breakfast, we went to hear mass. The morning passed off quickly, but towards dinner-time I thought that Christine looked different to what she did the day before, and I asked her the reason of that change.

"It must be," she said, "the same reason which causes you to be thoughtful."

"An air of thoughtfulness, my dear, is proper to love when it finds itself in consultation with honour. This affair has become serious, and love is now compelled to think and consider. We want to be married in the church, and we cannot do it before Lent, now that we are in the last days of carnival; yet we cannot wait until Easter, it would be too long. We must therefore obtain a dispensation in order to be married. Have I not reason to be thoughtful?"

Her only answer was to come and kiss me tenderly. I had spoken the truth, yet I had not told her all my reasons for being so pensive. I found myself drawn into an engagement which was not disagreeable to me, but I wished it had not been so very pressing. I could not conceal from myself that repentance was beginning to creep into my amorous and well-disposed mind, and I was grieved at it. I felt certain, however, that the charming girl would never have any cause to reproach me for her misery.

We had the whole evening before us, and as she had told me that she had never gone to a theatre, I resolved on affording her that pleasure. I sent for a Jew from whom I procured everything necessary to disguise her, and we went to the theatre. A man in love enjoys no pleasure but that which he gives to the woman he loves. After the performance was over, I took her to the Casino, and her astonishment made me laugh when she saw for the first time a faro bank. I had not money enough to play myself, but I had more than enough to amuse her and to let her play a reasonable game. I gave her ten sequins, and explained what she had to do. She did not even know the cards, yet in less than an hour she had won one hundred sequins. I made her leave off playing, and we returned to the inn. When we were in our room, I told her to see how much money she had, and when I assured her that all that gold belonged to her, she thought it was a dream.

"Oh! what will my uncle say?" she exclaimed.

We had a light supper, and spent a delightful night, taking good care to part by day-break, so as not to be caught in the same bed by the worthy ecclesiastic. He arrived early and found us sleeping soundly in our respective beds. He woke me, and I gave him the ring which he went to pledge immediately. When he returned two hours later, he saw us dressed and talking quietly near the fire. As soon as he came in, Christine rushed to embrace him, and she shewed him all the gold she had in her possession. What a pleasant surprise for the good old priest! He did not know how to express his wonder! He thanked God for what he called a miracle, and he concluded by saying that we were made to insure each other's happiness.

The time to part had come. I promised to pay them a visit in the first days of Lent, but on condition that on my arrival in P—— I would not find anyone informed of my name or of my concerns. The curate gave me the certificate of birth of his niece and the account of her possessions. As soon as they had gone I took my departure for Venice, full of love for the charming girl, and determined on keeping my engagement with her. I knew how easy it would be for me to convince my three friends that my marriage had been irrevocably written in the great book of fate.

My return caused the greatest joy to the three excellent men, because, not being accustomed to see me three days absent, M. Dandolo and M. Barbaro were afraid of some accident having befallen me; but M. de Bragadin's faith was stronger, and he allayed their fears, saying to them that, with Paralis watching over me, I could not be in any danger.

The very next day I resolved on insuring Christine's happiness without making her my wife. I had thought of marrying her when I loved her better than myself, but after obtaining possession the balance was so much on my side that my self-love proved stronger than my love for Christine. I could not make up my mind to renounce the advantages, the hopes which I thought were attached to my happy independence. Yet I was the slave of sentiment. To abandon the artless, innocent girl seemed to me an awful crime of which I could not be guilty, and the mere idea of it made me shudder. I was aware that she was, perhaps, bearing in her womb a living token of our mutual love, and I shivered at the bare possibility that her confidence in me might be repaid by shame and everlasting misery.

I bethought myself of finding her a husband in every way better than myself; a husband so good that she would not only forgive me for the insult I should thus be guilty of towards her, but also thank me at the end, and like me all the better for my deceit.

To find such a husband could not be very difficult, for Christine was not only blessed with wonderful beauty, and with a well-established reputation for virtue, but she was also the possessor of a fortune amounting to four thousand Venetian ducats.

Shut up in a room with the three worshippers of my oracle, I consulted Paralis upon the affair which I had so much at heart. The answer was:

"Serenus must attend to it."

Serenus was the cabalistic name of M. de Bragadin, and the excellent man immediately expressed himself ready to execute all the orders of Paralis. It was my duty to inform him of those orders.

"You must," I said to him, "obtain from the Holy Father a dispensation for a worthy and virtuous girl, so as to give her the privilege of marrying during Lent in the church of her village; she is a young country girl. Here is her certificate of birth. The husband is not yet known; but it does not matter, Paralis undertakes to find one."

"Trust to me," said my father, "I will write at once to our ambassador in Rome, and I will contrive to have my letter sent by special express. You need not be anxious, leave it all to me, I will make it a business of state, and I must obey Paralis all the more readily that I foresee that the intended husband is one of us four. Indeed, we must prepare ourselves to obey."

I had some trouble in keeping my laughter down, for it was in my power to metamorphose Christine into a grand Venetian lady, the wife of a senator; but that was not my intention. I again consulted the oracle in order to ascertain who would be the husband of the young girl, and the answer was that M. Dandolo was entrusted with the care of finding one, young, handsome, virtuous, and able to serve the Republic, either at home or abroad. M. Dandolo was to consult me before concluding any arrangements. I gave him courage for his task by informing him that the girl had a dowry of four thousand ducats, but I added that his choice was to be made within a fortnight. M. de Bragadin, delighted at not being entrusted with the commission, laughed heartily.

Those arrangements made me feel at peace with myself. I was certain that the husband I wanted would be found, and I only thought of finishing the carnival gaily, and of contriving to find my purse ready for a case of emergency.

Fortune soon rendered me possessor of a thousand sequins. I paid my debts, and the licence for the marriage having arrived from Rome ten days after M. de Bragadin had applied for it, I gave him one hundred ducats, that being the sum it had cost. The dispensation gave Christine the right of being married in any church in Christendom, she would only have to obtain the seal of the episcopal court of the diocese in which the marriage was to take place, and no publication of banns was required. We wanted, therefore, but one thing—a trifling one, namely, the husband. M. Dandolo had already proposed three or four to me, but I had refused them for excellent reasons. At last he offered one who suited me exactly.

I had to take the diamond ring out of pledge, and not wishing to do it myself, I wrote to the priest making an appointment in Treviso. I was not, of course, surprised when I found that he was accompanied by his lovely niece, who, thinking that I had come to complete all arrangements for our marriage, embraced me without ceremony, and I did the same. If the uncle had not been present, I am afraid that those kisses would have caused all my heroism to vanish. I gave the curate the dispensation, and the handsome features of Christine shone with joy. She certainly could not imagine that I had been working so actively for others, and, as I was not yet certain of anything, I did not undeceive her then. I promised to be in P—— within eight or ten days, when we would complete all necessary arrangements. After dinner, I gave the curate the ticket for the ring and the money to take it out of pledge, and we retired to rest. This time, very fortunately, there was but one bed in the room, and I had to take another chamber for myself.

The next morning, I went into Christine's room, and found her in bed. Her uncle had gone out for my diamond ring, and alone with that lovely girl, I found that I had, when necessary, complete control over my passions. Thinking that she was not to be my wife, and that she would belong to another, I considered it my duty to silence my desires. I kissed her, but nothing more.

I spent one hour with her, fighting like Saint Anthony against the carnal desires of my nature. I could see the charming girl full of love and of wonder at my reserve, and I admired her virtue in the natural modesty which prevented her from making the first advances. She got out of bed and dressed herself without shewing any disappointment. She would, of course, have felt mortified if she had had the slightest idea that I despised her, or that I did not value her charms.

Her uncle returned, gave me the ring, and we had dinner, after which he treated me to a wonderful exhibition. Christine had learned how to write, and, to give me a proof of her talent, she wrote very fluently and very prettily in my presence.

We parted, after my promising to come back again within ten days, and I returned to Venice.

On the second Sunday in Lent, M. Dandolo told me with an air of triumph that the fortunate husband had been found, and that there was no doubt of my approval of the new candidate. He named Charles— whom I knew by sight—very handsome young man, of irreproachable conduct, and about twenty-two years of age. He was clerk to M. Ragionato and god-son of Count Algarotti, a sister of whom had married M. Dandolo's brother.

"Charles," said M. Dandolo to me, "has lost his father and his mother, and I feel satisfied that his godfather will guarantee the dowry brought by his wife. I have spoken to him, and I believe him disposed to marry an honest girl whose dowry would enable him to purchase M. Ragionato's office."

"It seems to promise very well, but I cannot decide until I have seen him."

"I have invited him to dine with us to-morrow."

The young man came, and I found him worthy of all M. Dandolo's praise. We became friends at once; he had some taste for poetry, I read some of my productions to him, and having paid him a visit the following day, he shewed me several pieces of his own composition which were well written. He introduced me to his aunt, in whose house he lived with his sister, and I was much pleased with their friendly welcome. Being alone with him in his room, I asked him what he thought of love.

"I do not care for love," he answered: "but I should like to get married in order to have a house of my own."

When I returned to the palace, I told M. Dandolo that he might open the affair with Count Algarotti, and the count mentioned it to Charles, who said that he could not give any answer, either one way or the other, until he should have seen the young girl, talked with her, and enquired about her reputation. As for Count Algarotti, he was ready to be answerable for his god-son, that is to guarantee four thousand ducats to the wife, provided her dowry was worth that amount. Those were only the preliminaries; the rest belonged to my province.

Dandolo having informed Charles that the matter was entirely in my hands, he called on me and enquired when I would be kind enough to introduce him to the young person. I named the day, adding that it was necessary to devote a whole day to the visit, as she resided at a distance of twenty miles from Venice, that we would dine with her and return the same evening. He promised to be ready for me by day-break. I immediately sent an express to the curate to inform him of the day on which I would call with a friend of mine whom I wished to introduce to his niece.

On the appointed day, Charles was punctual. I took care to let him know along the road that I had made the acquaintance of the young girl and of her uncle as travelling companions from Venice to Mestra about one month before, and that I would have offered myself as a husband, if I had been in a position to guarantee the dowry of four thousand ducats. I did not think it necessary to go any further in my confidences.

We arrived at the good priest's house two hours before mid-day, and soon after our arrival, Christine came in with an air of great ease, expressing all her pleasure at seeing me. She only bowed to Charles, enquiring from me whether he was likewise a clerk.

Charles answered that he was clerk at Ragionato.

She pretended to understand, in order not to appear ignorant.

"I want you to look at my writing," she said to me, "and afterwards we will go and see my mother."

Delighted at the praise bestowed upon her writing by Charles, when he heard that she had learned only one month, she invited us to follow her. Charles asked her why she had waited until the age of nineteen to study writing.

"Well, sir, what does it matter to you? Besides, I must tell you that I am seventeen, and not nineteen years of age."

Charles entreated her to excuse him, smiling at the quickness of her answer.

She was dressed like a simple country girl, yet very neatly, and she wore her handsome gold chains round her neck and on her arms. I told her to take my arm and that of Charles, which she did, casting towards me a look of loving obedience. We went to her mother's house; the good woman was compelled to keep her bed owing to sciatica. As we entered the room, a respectable-looking man, who was seated near the patient, rose at the sight of Charles, and embraced him affectionately. I heard that he was the family physician, and the circumstance pleased me much.

After we had paid our compliments to the good woman, the doctor enquired after Charles's aunt and sister; and alluding to the sister who was suffering from a secret disease, Charles desired to say a few words to him in private; they left the room together. Being alone with the mother and Christine, I praised Charles, his excellent conduct, his high character, his business abilities, and extolled the happiness of the woman who would be his wife. They both confirmed my praises by saying that everything I said of him could be read on his features. I had no time to lose, so I told Christine to be on her guard during dinner, as Charles might possibly be the husband whom God had intended for her.

"For me?"

"Yes, for you. Charles is one of a thousand; you would be much happier with him than you could be with me; the doctor knows him, and you could ascertain from him everything which I cannot find time to tell you now about my friend."

The reader can imagine all I suffered in making this declaration, and my surprise when I saw the young girl calm and perfectly composed! Her composure dried the tears already gathering in my eyes. After a short silence, she asked me whether I was certain that such a handsome young man would have her. That question gave me an insight into Christine's heart and feelings, and quieted all my sorrow, for I saw that I had not known her well. I answered that, beautiful as she was, there was no doubt of her being loved by everybody.

"It will be at dinner, my dear Christine, that my friend will examine and study you; do not fail to shew all the charms and qualities with which God has endowed you, but do not let him suspect our intimacy."

"It is all very strange. Is my uncle informed of this wonderful change?"

"No."

"If your friend should feel pleased with me, when would he marry me?"

"Within ten days. I will take care of everything, and you will see me again in the course of the week."

Charles came back with the doctor, and Christine, leaving her mother's bedside, took a chair opposite to us. She answered very sensibly all the questions addressed to her by Charles, often exciting his mirth by her artlessness, but not shewing any silliness.

Oh! charming simplicity! offspring of wit and of ignorance! thy charm is delightful, and thou alone hast the privilege of saying anything without ever giving offence! But how unpleasant thou art when thou art not natural! and thou art the masterpiece of art when thou art imitated with perfection!

We dined rather late, and I took care not to speak to Christine, not even to look at her, so as not to engross her attention, which she devoted entirely to Charles, and I was delighted to see with what ease and interest she kept up the conversation. After dinner, and as we were taking leave, I heard the following words uttered by Charles, which went to my very heart:

"You are made, lovely Christine, to minister to the happiness of a prince."

And Christine? This was her answer:

"I should esteem myself fortunate, sir, if you should judge me worthy of ministering to yours."

These words excited Charles so much that he embraced me!

Christine was simple, but her artlessness did not come from her mind, only from her heart. The simplicity of mind is nothing but silliness, that of the heart is only ignorance and innocence; it is a quality which subsists even when the cause has ceased to be. This young girl, almost a child of nature, was simple in her manners, but graceful in a thousand trifling ways which cannot be described. She was sincere, because she did not know that to conceal some of our impressions is one of the precepts of propriety, and as her intentions were pure, she was a stranger to that false shame and mock modesty which cause pretended innocence to blush at a word, or at a movement said or made very often without any wicked purpose.

During our journey back to Venice Charles spoke of nothing but of his happiness. He had decidedly fallen in love.

"I will call to-morrow morning upon Count Algarotti," he said to me, "and you may write to the priest to come with all the necessary documents to make the contract of marriage which I long to sign."

His delight and his surprise were intense when I told him that my wedding present to Christine was a dispensation from the Pope for her to be married in Lent.

"Then," he exclaimed, "we must go full speed ahead!"

In the conference which was held the next day between my young substitute, his god-father, and M. Dandolo, it was decided that the parson should be invited to come with his niece. I undertook to carry the message, and leaving Venice two hours before morning I reached P—— early. The priest said he would be ready to start immediately after mass. I then called on Christine, and I treated her to a fatherly and sentimental sermon, every word of which was intended to point out to her the true road to happiness in the new condition which she was on the point of adopting. I told her how she ought to behave towards her husband, towards his aunt and his sister, in order to captivate their esteem and their love. The last part of my discourse was pathetic and rather disparaging to myself, for, as I enforced upon her the necessity of being faithful to her husband, I was necessarily led to entreat her pardon for having seduced her. "When you promised to marry me, after we had both been weak enough to give way to our love, did you intend to deceive me?"

"Certainly not."

"Then you have not deceived me. On the contrary, I owe you some gratitude for having thought that, if our union should prove unhappy, it was better to find another husband for me, and I thank God that you have succeeded so well. Tell me, now, what I can answer to your friend in case he should ask me, during the first night, why I am so different to what a virgin ought to be?"

"It is not likely that Charles, who is full of reserve and propriety, would ask you such a thing, but if he should, tell him positively that you never had a lover, and that you do not suppose yourself to be different to any other girl."

"Will he believe me?"

"He would deserve your contempt, and entail punishment on himself if he did not. But dismiss all anxiety; that will not occur. A sensible man, my dear Christine, when he has been rightly brought up, never ventures upon such a question, because he is not only certain to displease, but also sure that he will never know the truth, for if the truth is likely to injure a woman in the opinion of her husband, she would be very foolish, indeed, to confess it."

"I understand your meaning perfectly, my dear friend; let us, then, embrace each other for the last time."

"No, for we are alone and I am very weak. I adore thee as much as ever."

"Do not cry, dear friend, for, truly speaking, I have no wish for it."

That simple and candid answer changed my disposition suddenly, and, instead of crying, I began to laugh. Christine dressed herself splendidly, and after breakfast we left P——. We reached Venice in four hours. I lodged them at a good inn, and going to the palace, I told M. Dandolo that our people had arrived, that it would be his province to bring them and Charles together on the following day, and to attend to the matter altogether, because the honour of the future husband and wife, the respect due to their parents and to propriety, forbade any further interference on my part.

He understood my reasons, and acted accordingly. He brought Charles to me, I presented both of them to the curate and his niece, and then left them to complete their business.

I heard afterwards from M. Dandolo that they all called upon Count Algarotti, and at the office of a notary, where the contract of marriage was signed, and that, after fixing a day for the wedding, Charles had escorted his intended back to P——.

On his return, Charles paid me a visit. He told me that Christine had won by her beauty and pleasing manners the affection of his aunt, of his sister, and of his god-father, and that they had taken upon themselves all the expense of the wedding.

"We intend to be married," he added, "on such a day at P——, and I trust that you will crown your work of kindness by being present at the ceremony."

I tried to excuse myself, but he insisted with such a feeling of gratitude, and with so much earnestness, that I was compelled to accept. I listened with real pleasure to the account he gave me of the impression produced upon all his family and upon Count Algarotti by the beauty, the artlessness, the rich toilet, and especially by the simple talk of the lovely country girl.

"I am deeply in love with her," Charles said to me, "and I feel that it is to you that I shall be indebted for the happiness I am sure to enjoy with my charming wife. She will soon get rid of her country way of talking in Venice, because here envy and slander will but too easily shew her the absurdity of it."

His enthusiasm and happiness delighted me, and I congratulated myself upon my own work. Yet I felt inwardly some jealousy, and I could not help envying a lot which I might have kept for myself.

M. Daridolo and M. Barbaro having been also invited by Charles, I went with them to P——. We found the dinner-table laid out in the rector's house by the servants of Count Algarotti, who was acting as Charles's father, and having taken upon himself all the expense of the wedding, had sent his cook and his major-domo to P——.

When I saw Christine, the tears filled my eyes, and I had to leave the room. She was dressed as a country girl, but looked as lovely as a nymph. Her husband, her uncle, and Count Algarotti had vainly tried to make her adopt the Venetian costume, but she had very wisely refused.

"As soon as I am your wife," she had said to Charles, "I will dress as you please, but here I will not appear before my young companions in any other costume than the one in which they have always seen me. I shall thus avoid being laughed at, and accused of pride, by the girls among whom I have been brought up."

There was in these words something so noble, so just, and so generous, that Charles thought his sweetheart a supernatural being. He told me that he had enquired, from the woman with whom Christine had spent a fortnight, about the offers of marriage she had refused at that time, and that he had been much surprised, for two of those offers were excellent ones.

"Christine," he added, "was evidently destined by Heaven for my happiness, and to you I am indebted for the precious possession of that treasure."

His gratitude pleased me, and I must render myself the justice of saying that I entertained no thought of abusing it. I felt happy in the happiness I had thus given.

We repaired to the church towards eleven o'clock, and were very much astonished at the difficulty we experienced in getting in. A large number of the nobility of Treviso, curious to ascertain whether it was true that the marriage ceremony of a country girl would be publicly performed during Lent when, by waiting only one month, a dispensation would have been useless, had come to P——. Everyone wondered at the permission having been obtained from the Pope, everyone imagined that there was some extraordinary reason for it, and was in despair because it was impossible to guess that reason. In spite of all feelings of envy, every face beamed with pleasure and satisfaction when the young couple made their appearance, and no one could deny that they deserved that extraordinary distinction, that exception to all established rules.

A certain Countess of Tos, . . . from Treviso, Christine's god-mother, went up to her after the ceremony, and embraced her most tenderly, complaining that the happy event had not been communicated to her in Treviso. Christine, in her artless way, answered with as much modesty as sweetness, that the countess ought to forgive her if she had failed in her duty towards her, on account of the marriage having been decided on so hastily. She presented her husband, and begged Count Algarotti to atone for her error towards her god-mother by inviting her to join the wedding repast, an invitation which the countess accepted with great pleasure. That behaviour, which is usually the result of a good education and a long experience of society, was in the lovely peasant-girl due only to a candid and well-balanced mind which shone all the more because it was all nature and not art.

As they returned from the church, Charles and Christine knelt down before the young wife's mother, who gave them her blessing with tears of joy.

Dinner was served, and, of course, Christine and her happy spouse took the seats of honour. Mine was the last, and I was very glad of it, but although everything was delicious, I ate very little, and scarcely opened my lips.

Christine was constantly busy, saying pretty things to every one of her guests, and looking at her husband to make sure that he was pleased with her.

Once or twice she addressed his aunt and sister in such a gracious manner that they could not help leaving their places and kissing her tenderly, congratulating Charles upon his good fortune. I was seated not very far from Count Algarotti, and I heard him say several times to Christine's god-mother that he had never felt so delighted in his life.

When four o'clock struck, Charles whispered a few words to his lovely wife, she bowed to her god-mother, and everybody rose from the table. After the usual compliments—and in this case they bore the stamp of sincerity—the bride distributed among all the girls of the village, who were in the adjoining room, packets full of sugar-plums which had been prepared before hand, and she took leave of them, kissing them all without any pride. Count Algarotti invited all the guests to sleep at a house he had in Treviso, and to partake there of the dinner usually given the day after the wedding. The uncle alone excused himself, and the mother could not come, owing to her disease which prevented her from moving. The good woman died three months after Christine's marriage.

Christine therefore left her village to follow her husband, and for the remainder of their lives they lived together in mutual happiness.

Count Algarotti, Christine's god-mother and my two noble friends, went away together. The bride and bridegroom had, of course, a carriage to themselves, and I kept the aunt and the sister of Charles company in another. I could not help envying the happy man somewhat, although in my inmost heart I felt pleased with his happiness.

The sister was not without merit. She was a young widow of twenty-five, and still deserved the homage of men, but I gave the preference to the aunt, who told me that her new niece was a treasure, a jewel which was worthy of everybody's admiration, but that she would not let her go into society until she could speak the Venetian dialect well.

"Her cheerful spirits," she added, "her artless simplicity, her natural wit, are like her beauty, they must be dressed in the Venetian fashion. We are highly pleased with my nephew's choice, and he has incurred everlasting obligations towards you. I hope that for the future you will consider our house as your own."

The invitation was polite, perhaps it was sincere, yet I did not avail myself of it, and they were glad of it. At the end of one year Christine presented her husband with a living token of their mutual love, and that circumstance increased their conjugal felicity.

We all found comfortable quarters in the count's house in Treviso, where, after partaking of some refreshments, the guests retired to rest.

The next morning I was with Count Algarotti and my two friends when Charles came in, handsome, bright, and radiant. While he was answering with much wit some jokes of the count, I kept looking at him with some anxiety, but he came up to me and embraced me warmly. I confess that a kiss never made me happier.

People wonder at the devout scoundrels who call upon their saint when they think themselves in need of heavenly assistance, or who thank him when they imagine that they have obtained some favour from him, but people are wrong, for it is a good and right feeling, which preaches against Atheism.

At the invitation of Charles, his aunt and his sister had gone to pay a morning visit to the young wife, and they returned with her. Happiness never shone on a more lovely face!

M. Algarotti, going towards her, enquired from her affectionately whether she had had a good night. Her only answer was to rush to her husband's arms. It was the most artless, and at the same time the most eloquent, answer she could possible give. Then turning her beautiful eyes towards me, and offering me her hand, she said,

"M. Casanova, I am happy, and I love to be indebted to you for my happiness."

The tears which were flowing from my eyes, as I kissed her hand, told her better than words how truly happy I was myself.

The dinner passed off delightfully. We then left for Mestra and Venice. We escorted the married couple to their house, and returned home to amuse M. Bragadin with the relation of our expedition. This worthy and particularly learned man said a thousand things about the marriage, some of great profundity and others of great absurdity.

I laughed inwardly. I was the only one who had the key to the mystery, and could realize the secret of the comedy.

A Note About the Author

Giacomo Casanova (1725–1798) was an Italian adventurer and author. Born in Venice, Casanova was the eldest of six siblings born to Gaetano Casanova and Zanetta Farussi, an actor and actress. Raised in a city noted for its cosmopolitanism, night life, and glamor, Casanova overcame a sickly childhood to excel in school, entering the University of Padua at the age of 12. After graduating in 1742 with a degree in law, he struggled to balance his work as a lawyer and low-level cleric with a growing gambling addiction. As scandals and a prison sentence threatened to derail his career in the church, Casanova managed to find work as a scribe for a powerful Cardinal in Rome, but was soon dismissed and entered military service for the Republic of Venice. Over the next several years, he left the service, succeeded as a professional gambler, and embarked on a Grand Tour of Europe. Towards the end of his life, Casanova worked on his exhaustive, scandalous memoirs, a 12-volume autobiography reflecting on a legendary life of romance and debauchery that brought him from the heights of aristocratic society to the lows of illness and imprisonment. Recognized for his self-styled sensationalism as much as he is for his detailed chronicling of 18th century European culture, Casanova is a man whose name is now synonymous with the kind of life he led—fast, fearless, and free.

A Note from the Publisher

Spanning many genres, from non-fiction essays to literature classics to children's books and lyric poetry, Mint Edition books showcase the master works of our time in a modern new package. The text is freshly typeset, is clean and easy to read, and features a new note about the author in each volume. Many books also include exclusive new introductory material. Every book boasts a striking new cover, which makes it as appropriate for collecting as it is for gift giving. Mint Edition books are only printed when a reader orders them, so natural resources are not wasted. We're proud that our books are never manufactured in excess and exist only in the exact quantity they need to be read and enjoyed.

bookfinity™

Discover more of your favorite classics with Bookfinity™.

- Track your reading with custom book lists.
- Get great book recommendations for your personalized Reader Type.
- Add reviews for your favorite books.
- AND MUCH MORE!

Visit **bookfinity.com** and take the fun Reader Type quiz to get started.

Enjoy our classic and modern companion pairings!

Classic & Modern

www.ingramcontent.com/pod-product-compliance
Lightning Source LLC
Chambersburg PA
CBHW021136020426
42331CB00005B/801